handmade *hellos*

handmade *hellos*

Fresh Greeting Card Projects from First-Rate Crafters

Written and edited by Eunice Moyle *and* Sabrina Moyle

Photographs by Sheri Giblin • Illustrations by Sarah Labieniec

CHRONICLE BOOKS

SAN FRANCISCO

Library of Congress Cataloging-in-Publication Data

Moyle, Eunice.

Handmade hellos : fresh greeting card projects from first-rate crafters /
written and edited by Eunice Moyle and Sabrina Moyle ;
illustrations by Sarah Labieniec ; photographs by Sheri Giblin.

      p. cm.
  Includes index.
  ISBN: 978-0-8118-6239-4
  1. Greeting cards. I. Moyle, Sabrina. II. Title.

  TT872.M69 2008

  745.594'1—dc22

                        2007042617

Manufactured in China

Designed by Sara Gillingham.
Typesetting by Janis Reed.

10 9 8 7 6 5 4 3 2 1

Chronicle Books LLC
680 Second Street
San Francisco, California 94107

www.chroniclebooks.com

Adobe Photoshop and Adobe Illustrator are registered trademarks of Adobe
Systems Inc. Dahle is a registered trademark of Wilhelm Dahle Buro-technik
GMBH & Co. eBay is a registered trademark of eBay Inc. Fiskars is a registered
trademark of Fiskars Brands Inc. Liberty of London is a registered trademark
of the Liberty Public Limited Co. Macintosh is a registered trademark of Apple
Computer Inc. Microsoft Word is a registered trademark of the Microsoft
Corp. Mod Podge is a registered trademark of the Enterprise Paint Manufac-
turing Co. Mylar is a registered trademark of E. I. DuPont DeNemours and
Co. Osborne & Little is a registered trademark of the Osborne & Little PLC
Corp. Polaroid is a registered trademark of the Polaroid Corp. Print Gocco is
a registered Trademark of the Riso Kagaku Corp. Scotch Tape is a registered
trademark of the 3M Co. Sesame Street is a registered trademark of Children's
Television Workshop. Stylist is a registered trademark of KSIN Luxembourg III,
S.A.R.L. X-Acto is a registered trademark of Elmer's Products, Inc.

To our mom and dad,
and to
Julian and Daniel.

contents

Introduction 6

How to Use This Book 7

Projects

We grew up in Asia and traveled the world from the time we were two years old; our mom was a domestic goddess and our dad was a diplomat. As far back as we can remember, we were surrounded by artisan objects from around the world—embroidered smocks, quilts, ceramics, and, of course, handcrafted cards.

We especially remember the wonderful cut-paper cards we used to find at street fairs growing up in China. Colorful, intricate scenes of dragons, phoenixes, horses, and tigers hand-cut from diaphanous tissue paper and glued daintily to a piece of card stock. Back in the United States, we remember discovering the wonderful, graphic woodblock print cards of nature scenes (everything from lizards to spider monkeys) that our biologist Aunt Ginny made for special occasions.

Years later, we channeled our love of handcrafted goods into starting Hello!Lucky, a small stationery company specializing in making cards and invitations the old-fashioned way, using vintage letterpress printing presses from the 1950s. To this day, our favorite pastime is brainstorming new card ideas, making them ourselves, and watching the delighted reactions of the people who receive them. There is nothing more satisfying in the world!

Hello!Lucky has also allowed us to join a vibrant artistic community of like-minded crafters who have chosen paper goods as their medium. Like us, these artists, many of whom contributed the wonderful projects in this book, create their own cards from start to finish using hands-on, labor-intensive techniques (read more about the artists at the end of each project). As you make your own cards, we encourage you to seek out the work of these artists for ideas and inspiration!

introduction

The genius of a handmade card is that it's truly personal.

Sure, professionally printed cards are convenient, but quite often that airbrushed flower bouquet paired with the rhyming verse misses the mark completely. So many occasions—from a new home to an old joke, a big birthday to a small raise—deserve nothing short of a personal tribute. This is when you need something much more special than a mass-produced greeting card.

You can tailor everything about a handmade card, from design to words, to reflect the personalities of both you and your card's recipient. Buttons. Balsa wood. Fabric scraps. Thumbprints. Thread. Googly eyes. Newspaper horoscopes. You can make creative cards using all kinds of unexpected materials, many of which you may already have around your home; other materials you can find at your local craft store. The abundance and affordability of supplies are a huge part of why we love making cards by hand—why buy a $9, albeit charming, birthday card from a boutique when you can achieve the same "awww" factor yourself for next to nothing?

Plus, handmade cards are incredibly easy to make. Unlike, say, knitting a sweater or embroidering a caftan, making a card doesn't require studying a series of precise techniques. Trust us, you will never be forced to give someone a half-made card with a plaintive disclaimer saying, *I promise to finish this within the decade.* When you start one of our card projects, we promise you'll finish it in a few hours or less so you can revel in the praise and adoration of the card's lucky recipient.

Card making is something that can be part of your everyday life, whether you're a hip urbanite or a sassy suburban mom. It's a way to slow down, appreciate good times, and exercise your creative side. Even if the last card you made involved turning your traced hand into a turkey, there's a project here that's perfectly suited for your skill level and style. To get the best variety, we tapped our favorite artists from all over the world for their favorite card-making techniques. You'll learn how to collage, screen print, make pop-ups, string a garland, use a Print Gocco machine, bind a booklet, embroider, emboss, stamp, stencil, and so much more. And all of the artists bring a unique fashion to their card, whether it's sweet, snarky, kitschy, or elegant. And, of course, we made sure the projects span every occasion and sentiment—from thank you to thinking of you, sympathy to save the date, happy birthday to holiday cheer—so you're never at a loss for words.

So, go ahead, get started!

how to use this book

The 27 main projects in this book involve a variety of materials and encompass many important occasions. The order in which you attempt the projects is completely up to you, though if you are less experienced working with paper, we suggest starting with an easy project to get yourself going.

Each project includes a list of ingredients and detailed how-to instructions and illustrations. Where stencils and templates are required, you'll find them in an envelope at the back of the book. A list of Resources (page 139) for finding specialized materials also is included. Refer to the Materials, Tools, and Techniques section (page 131) to familiarize yourself with some commonly used card-making materials and methods. You may also use that section as a quick reference for lingo, such as *bone folder, brayer,* and *Gocco.*

And don't miss the Variations section we've added to the end of most of the projects. There, you'll find many ideas to adapt the techniques from that project to make the card fit different occasions—it's like getting 84 project ideas in all!

MAKING THE GRADE (AND THE TIME!)

Each project has been graded in terms of difficulty level, which also tends to indicate how much time will be required to make that card. Here's what you can expect from those grades:

Basic: These projects are easy to make and require little practice or skill. Typically, these cards will take fewer than 30 minutes to create. These are great projects to make with kids!

Moderate: These projects require a bit more focus and concentration. Some

MAKING CARDS WITH KIDS

Card making is a great creative project for a Sunday afternoon with kids. The easier projects require few skills and only a small attention span and can help teach etiquette, the value of personal expression, and the strength of the written word. We especially recommend the following projects for kids: **Owl-y Friend** (page 17), **Lacy Paper Notes** (page 43), **Fuzzy Octopus Valentine** (page 121), **Humpty Dumpty Thumbprint Card** (page 75), **Pop-Up Birdie Hello** (page 31), and **Ahoy There! Pop-Up Pirate Card** (page 125). Just remember to substitute safety scissors wherever a utility knife is suggested, and watch out for small objects such as googly eyes!

Despite being made of paper, cards don't have to be harmful to the environment. Use post consumer-waste recycled paper or scrap paper in your cards and consider encouraging recipients to recycle their cards with a small *recycle me!* stamp on the back. See the Ecofriendly Papers resource list on page 139.

cards may involve a greater number of steps and techniques, such as sewing buttons or tracing a stencil. Cards with this grade may typically be made in 1–2 hours.

Advanced: These projects are for the motivated card maker. They require a bit more patience and hand–eye coordination; they also sometimes entail learning a multistep technique, such as block printing, or using a new tool, like a silk-screening kit (and thus having to read the manufacturer's instruction manual!). Plan to set aside at least an afternoon to complete these cards, but be prepared to reap the rewards of a fabulous new skill that you'll be able to deploy on many a future occasion!

Note: If a project is marked Advanced, don't despair! Often, we suggest an easier version of the project in the Variations section, which you'll find at the end of the instructions.

GET READY . . .

While each project provides a detailed list of the tools you'll need to complete it, the following items should be staples in your card-making tool kit. Having these on hand will help you hit the ground running and minimize trips to the craft store:

- *Card stock or blank cards.* Many of the projects start with a flat or folded blank card. Keep a supply of heavyweight card stock handy in a variety of colors, ranging from light to bold. Throw some iridescent card stock in the mix for occasions that call for extra pizzazz. Alternatively, many craft stores sell ready-made blank cards; purchase these to save time on trimming, scoring, and folding.

- *Envelopes.* You'll need these to mail your cards, so keep a stash on hand in different colors and sizes. You can also make your own out of text-weight paper (see page 136).

- *Text-weight paper.* Gather a range of text-weight paper, including colorful solids and pretty patterns, for adding embellishments to the cards.

- *Ruler.* This will come in handy for trimming down card stock and scoring your cards. We recommend getting a cork-backed metal ruler, which provides a firm grip for cutting straight lines with your utility knife. In addition, a metal triangle speeds up trimming right angles.

- *Utility or craft knife.* A utility knife, used in combination with your cork-backed ruler, is the ideal way to get clean, straight lines when trimming cards. Keep extra blades on hand to ensure clean cuts every time.

- *Bone folder.* This nifty bookbinding tool is indispensable for getting clean creases and folds.

- *Cutting mat.* While a cutting mat is not essential, it keeps you from damaging your work surface. Cutting mats are typically printed with a measuring grid, which can eliminate the need for a ruler. If you're not ready to invest, a magazine works well, too.

- *Scissors.* Have scissors on hand for cutting odd shapes and curves. Keep safety scissors on hand if you're working with kids and want to avoid using a utility knife.

- *Glue stick or double-sided tape.* Most of the projects involve gluing stuff together, for which a glue stick is nice and neat. You may also use double-sided tape.

- *Rubber-stamp alphabet kit and ink pad.* When it's time to put a greeting on the front of your card, a rubber-stamp alphabet kit works well and keeps things looking neat and tidy.

GET SET . . .

Most of the projects require that you start with either a flat or a folded card. For a flat card, simply trim your card stock to size using a utility knife, ruler, and cutting mat (or a ruler, pencil, and scissors).

For a folded card, there is the added step of putting a good crease and fold in the middle of the card. There are a couple of tricks to doing this:

- *Find the grain.* The grain is the direction in which the paper fibers run. Folding with the grain results in a smooth, sturdy fold. If folded against the grain, some papers will crack or even tear. The easiest way to find the grain is through trial and error, and by looking closely at how the paper behaves at the fold.

- *Score, then fold.* The secret to a good, clean fold is to score the card first using a ruler and bone folder. First, measure and mark the halfway point at the top and bottom of your card. Align a ruler along the marks (the ruler should be going against the grain), and run your bone folder along the edge, creating a nice crease. Fold your card, and run your bone folder along the spine to reinforce the fold.

- *Make sure it fits.* There's nothing worse than making a fabulous card and realizing it won't fit in your envelope (or that it swims around inside it). A finished card should be about $1/8$" smaller than your envelope on all sides and should slide easily in and out. If your card has more than one fold or has embellishments, such as buttons or googly eyes, you'll need to factor in a little extra room.

PAPER SIZES **1 inch = 2.54 cm**

U.S. Paper Size	European Paper Size
11 x 17"	A3 (29.7 x 42 cm)
Letter ($8^1/_2$ x 11")	A4 (21 x 29.7 cm)

CARD AND ENVELOPE SIZES

U.S. Card Size	U.S. Envelope Size	European Card Size	European Envelope Size
A7 (5 x 7")	A7 ($5^1/_4$ x $7^1/_4$")	A5—half A4—(14.8 x 21 cm)	C5 (16.2 x 22.9 cm)
A6 ($4^1/_2$ x $6^1/_4$")	A6 ($4^3/_4$ x $6^1/_2$")	A6—half A5—(10.5 x 14.8 cm)	C6 (11.4 x 16.2 cm)
A2 ($4^1/_4$ x $5^1/_2$")	A2 ($4^3/_8$ x $5^3/_4$")	NA—Substitute A6	NA—Substitute C6
4-bar ($3^1/_2$ x $4^7/_8$")	4-bar ($3^5/_8$ x $5^1/_8$")	A7—half A6—(7.4 x 10.5 cm)	C7 (8.1 x 11.4 cm)

projects

To: Mr Punchinello
No. 3 Scrabble rd.
Cheshire Ch "MN
England

Post fra Ingrid!

special delivery self-mailing note

Darling Clementine

you'll need

Utility knife

Ruler

Cutting mat, or a magazine

Pretty, patterned text-weight paper (trimmed to 9 x 12¹/₂")

Pen(s) or rubber-stamp alphabet kit

2 mailing labels or paper and a glue stick for making labels

Scissors

Decorative paper punch (optional)

These origami notes are sweet, simple, and, housed in their ready-to-mail envelopes, totally ingenious. The patterned paper exterior will stand out instantly in the ho-hum torrent of regular mail. And unfolding one is like opening a gift, unleashing that giddy flutter of anticipation. Now, that's the kind of attention a handmade, hand-written card deserves!

how to:

1 Trim the paper to size.

Using your utility knife, ruler, and cutting mat, trim the paper to a rectangle measuring 9 x 12¹/₂".

2 Fold the paper into an envelope.

Fold the rectangle in half widthwise to create a centerline, making sure the fold is parallel to the shorter side (Figure 1). Unfold the rectangle. Fold the upper right corner in so that the top edge folds down to meet the centerline (Figure 2). Fold the bottom left corner in to meet the centerline in the same manner (Figure 3). Fold the bottom right edge of your paper up to meet the bottom edge of your first fold. Repeat, this time folding the top left edge down (Figure 4). Take the bottom right corner and fold it up

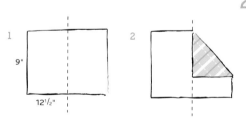

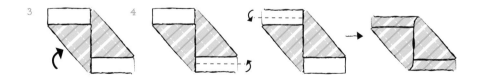

so that the bottom edge meets the centerline (Figure 5). Fold the top left corner down to meet the centerline. Underneath the tips of the right and left flaps you have just created, you will see a little triangle. Tuck each tip under the corresponding triangle when you are ready to close your envelope (Figure 6).

3 Write a note.

Before closing the envelope, you'll want to write your message. Unfold the envelope and write the message in the rectangular area created by your folds. (Use light-colored ink so it doesn't show through on the outside of the envelope.)

4 Close and address the envelope.

Fold your envelope back up and tuck in the flaps. Apply a mailing label to the front, or trim out your own label and address it using pens or rubber stamps. The labels shown here were trimmed with scissors at two corners, echoing the shape of the envelope (Figure 7).

5 Seal the envelope.

Apply a second label to the back of the envelope to keep it from opening in the mail (optional). Decorate this label using pens or rubber stamps, and/or write your return address here. Consider using a decorative paper punch, available at most art-supply stores, to add a little flair to your labels.

variations:

Size it up (or down). You can create your origami note out of any size rectangular paper. The larger the sheet, the larger the envelope and writing area will be. (A 9 x 12$\frac{1}{2}$" sheet of paper yields a 6$\frac{1}{4}$ x 4$\frac{1}{4}$" card; an 8$\frac{1}{2}$ x 11" sheet of paper yields a 5$\frac{3}{4}$ x 3$\frac{1}{2}$" card; and a 7 x 10" sheet of paper yields a 4$\frac{3}{4}$ x 3$\frac{3}{8}$" card.)

Add a card. Have a lot to say? Cut a rectangle of paper or card stock, and lay it inside your envelope. Trim down the upper right and lower left corners to match the shape of the writing area. Mix and match by using a solid paper in a contrasting color or a complementary patterned sheet.

Mount a photo. Turn your note into a fabulous photo birth announcement or holiday card by mounting a photo inside (remember to choose the patterned paper accordingly!). You can reduce or enlarge the size of your card (see above) to fit any size photo.

Place the photo inside the card, and mark the top right and lower left corners with a pencil. Cut a slit diagonal to the two corners using a utility knife. Make the slits just wide enough that the photo corners can be tucked in, holding the photo securely in place.

Or, just include the photo. If mounting it is too much work, just place a loose photo inside the card and write your message in the usual place.

Name:

Darling Clementine

(Tonje Holand and Ingrid Reithaug)

Location: Oslo, Norway

How did you get into crafting and/or card making? We graduated with degrees in graphic design and have since pursued our love for print- and card-making with the mutual idea of creating something new and innovative.

What is your favorite medium? We love working with paper, obviously, but the best results often come when adding new features, such as hand-stamped illustrations or bits of textiles.

What is the most memorable card you've ever received (or sent)? All cards that we can tell the sender put thought and effort into creating, just for us!

What is your favorite card-sending occasion? When there is no real occasion at all.

What is the one crafting tool you can't live without? Though we started out making cards by hand, we now print our work on a larger scale. This means a Macintosh computer is our most important tool.

What most inspires your work? The '20s and '40s, cocktail cherries, red helium balloons, art deco, Czech animation, cupcakes, camping, old toys, paper dolls, Polaroid photos, Bauhaus, and things made out of felt.

What Web site is your favorite source of inspiration? http://designsponge.blogspot.com/, www.sukie.co.uk, and www.fionahewitt.com.

Where can we find you on the Web? www.darlingclementine.no and www.darlingclem.blogspot.com.

Petra Boase

owl-y friend MODERATE

A wise and quirky bird, this owl is the perfect ambassador for all your wit and wisdom. We especially love the layering of patterned papers, buttons, and, of course, the googly eyes. It's the perfect card to whip up last minute using scraps and materials you already have on hand.

you'll need

Scissors

Owl-y Friend templates

Pencil (for tracing)

6 to 8 pieces of paper or fabric, roughly 5 x 7" per piece

Glue stick

4½ x 6½" folded card

2 googly eyes

2 buttons

how to:

1 **Trace and cut the owl.**

Start with a blank folded card (Figure 1). Cut out the Owl-y Friend templates (Figure 2). Trace the pieces of the template onto your selected papers and fabrics, choosing different patterns for each body part or doing them monochromatically, whichever you prefer. Make sure to place the papers and fabrics facedown when tracing so that your trace marks don't show on the finished card.

2 **Cut and adhere the background.**

Select a paper or fabric for your background and trim to a size equal to or somewhat smaller than the front of your card—no need to be precise, a little crookedness adds to the charm of this card. Apply glue to the wrong side of the background piece and adhere the piece to the front of your card (Figure 3).

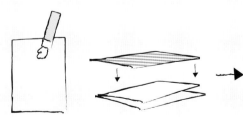

4

Name:
Petra Boase

Location: Norfolk, United Kingdom

How did you get into crafting and/or card making? By accident, really. My old studio in London had open weekends twice a year, so I would whip up a load of cards. They kept selling, and the rest is history!

What is your favorite medium? Old fabrics, appliqué, and Adobe Photoshop and Illustrator.

What is the most memorable card you've ever received (or sent)? My granny's birthday post-office specials are always a source of entertainment.

What is your favorite card-sending occasion? Valentine's Day.

What is the one crafting tool you can't live without? Hot-glue gun.

What things most inspire your work? Foreign flea markets and nostalgia.

What Web site is your favorite source of inspiration? www.etsy.com.

Where can we find you on the Web? www.petraboaseshop.com.

3 Add the owl.
Apply glue to the wrong sides of the various parts of your owl and stick the pieces to the card, starting with the body and layering pieces on top. Apply glue to the wrong side of the googly eyes and adhere (Figure 4).

4 Embellish the card.
Cut out freestyle branch and flower shapes from a paper or fabric of your choice, or use the templates provided. Apply glue to the wrong sides and adhere the branch and then the flowers to the card. Apply glue to the backs of your buttons and center them on the flowers, pressing firmly to adhere. Set the card aside for about 30 minutes, or until the glue is completely dry.

variations:

Child's birthday. Kids are sure to love this card, so consider making one for a little friend's birthday. (Just make sure the child is old enough that the googly eyes and buttons don't present a choking hazard.)

Wise, old owl. The owl is known to symbolize wisdom. Think about giving this card for a graduation or birthday (older and wiser!).

Spooky owl. Choose black and orange papers or fabrics and transform this into a fabulous Halloween card. Add a full moon to the background by cutting a circle out of yellow construction paper or fabric.

Whoo loves you? Make this card out of pink and red papers or fabrics. If puns are your thing, add the irresistible caption.

Snow owl. Make your owl out of winter-white or glittery papers or fabrics for a fresh and festive holiday greeting.

everyday fabric collage card BASIC

5 x 7" card stock in 2 to 3 different colors

Utility knife

Ruler

Cutting mat, or a magazine

Corner rounder, or a glass to use as a guide for rounding corners (optional)

Iron

Double-sided fusible web, close in weight to that of the fabric you are using (see Resources, page 139)

Scraps of fabric (we recommend lightweight fabrics, such as cotton prints)

Scissors

Glue stick

These chic, retro cards use scraps of vintage-inspired fabrics to create a simple, modern collage. We especially love using scraps of sturdy, cotton quilting fabrics, which quilting shops often sell in bundles. Little finishes like a colorful border and rounded corners add texture and make this card an extra-special treat.

how to:

1   Cut the card stock.
Select the card-stock color you'd like to use for the backing of your card, and trim it (using your utility knife, ruler, and cutting mat) so that it is $1/8$" smaller than your envelope on all sides. (In the example shown on page 20, the card is $4^1/2$ x $6^1/4$".) This is Card 1 (Figure 1). Cut contrasting card stock $1/8$" smaller than Card 1 on all sides. This is Card 2 (Figure 2). Card 2 will sit on top of Card 1, revealing a nice border around all edges (Figure 3). If you'd like, round the corners of both pieces of card stock: to get symmetrically rounded edges, use a corner rounder, or place the bottom of a glass at each corner of your card and trace the curve using a utility knife.

2   Add fusible web to the fabric.
Iron fusible web onto the wrong side of the fabric you'd like to use for your leaves and branch; set the iron to medium heat with no steam, or use it according to the manufacturer's instructions (Figure 4).

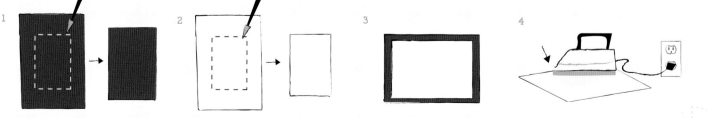

3 Cut the fabric into shapes.

Cut out free-form leaf shapes and a strip or several strips for your branches and/or trunk (Figure 5). You can always practice by cutting your shapes out of paper first; when you achieve a shape you like, use it as a stencil to cut your fabric.

4 Attach the fabric to the card, and glue the cards together.

Peel the fusible web backing from your fabric shapes. Arrange the shapes onto Card 2. Start with the trunk and then add leaves as you like, affixing your shapes in place using an iron on medium heat with no steam (Figure 6). Apply glue to the back of Card 2, spreading evenly to the outside edges. Center Card 2 onto Card 1 and press to adhere (Figure 7).

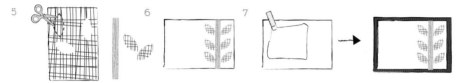

variations:

This card is limited only by your imagination and ability to cut shapes out of fabric!

Brilliant borders. Create a tiered border by layering a colorful card between two cards of a contrasting (lighter or darker) color. During Step 1: Choose a colorful card stock and use this as Card 2. Cut a third card ⅛" smaller on all sides than Card 2. This is Card 3. Follow Steps 2–4 above, but affix your fabric shapes to Card 3. Glue the cards together in the following order: 1, 2, 3!

Jolly dots. This variation sandwiches the fabric between two cards, rather than fusing it to the top card, and calls for a circle cutter, but you can also use circular scrapbooking punches, or just trace the base of a small jar or bottle and then cut out the shape using scissors or a utility knife. Or, if you're not feeling adventurous, just try a series of squares or rectangles!

Follow Step 1 from the main instructions. Then, using a circle cutter, cut out a random group of circles from Card 2. Cut fabric scraps a little larger than the circles you cut from Card 2. Spread glue on the back of Card 2. Place fabric scraps in corresponding circle holes, wrong side up. Place Card 2 onto Card 1. Press, and let dry.

Name:

Shim + Sons

(Sally J. Shim)

Location: Portland, Oregon

How did you get into crafting and/or card making? Colored pencils, scissors, and glue were my prized possessions as a young child. During graduate school, I designed bridal shower and baby shower invitations for friends and family. A few years later, I started a small custom stationery design business.

What is your favorite medium? Fabric and paper.

What is the most memorable card you've ever received (or sent)? A box full of handwritten cards my husband gave me while we were dating will always hold special memories.

What is your favorite card-sending occasion? Christmas. It is probably the only time that I am able to sit down and design something with the recipients in mind.

What is the one crafting tool you can't live without? My Dahle paper cutter. I use it every day!

What things most inspire your work? Organic shapes and patterns found in nature, simple and clean lines in modern architecture, craft blogs, design Web sites, Japanese craft books, and magazines.

What Web site is your favorite source of inspiration? www.flickr.com.

Where can we find you on the Web? www.shimandsons.etsy.com.

paper portrait friendship card `ADVANCED`

you'll need

Photo of a friend or family member

Photocopier

Pencil

Two 8½ x 11" sheets of tracing paper

4 to 6 assorted sheets of text-weight paper in solid colors (including a color that matches your loved one's skin tone) for making the face

Utility knife

Ruler

Cutting mat, or a magazine

Glue stick

Bone folder

4½ x 6¼" folded card

Ballpoint pen

With its singular focus on a loved-one's face, this makes a great birthday card, valentine, or thinking-of-you card. It's also the perfect way to commemorate a big achievement, promotion, or feat of unusual daring. Plus, it lets those of us who aren't born artists easily achieve a stunning rendering of a dear friend.

how to:

1 Photocopy the picture.

Make a black-and-white photocopy of your photo, reducing or enlarging it as necessary to fit the size card you want to make. Decide which elements of the photo really define your friend's face, and crop or center the photocopy around those details. In this example, the card focuses on her haircut, plump lips, big eyes, and rosy cheeks.

2 Trace the photo.

Using a pencil and tracing paper, trace the outer edges of the head and neck, as well as any other details you would like to include (Figure 1). In the example on page 22, we ignored her clothes and created a rounded, silhouette-like neckline to keep things simple. Set the tracing aside until Step 4; this will be the template you'll use to help guide the placement of the cutout features. Take a second sheet of tracing paper and repeat, this time tracing each element onto a separate area of paper (Figure 2); you will be cutting out each element in the next step.

1 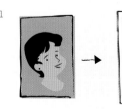 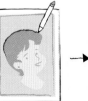 2

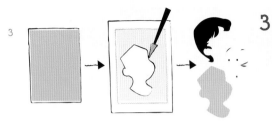

3 Cut out the features.

Choose a text-weight paper that matches your friend's skin tone. Place your tracing of the head and neck onto your paper, right side up, and cut the shape out with your utility knife, cutting through both the tracing paper and text-weight paper. Repeat for the hair, shirt collar, or any other details you have traced, choosing appropriate paper colors for each (Figure 3).

4 Attach the head, neck, and remaining features to the front of the card.

Apply glue to the back of the head-and-neck cutout, and center the piece on the front of your card, smoothing it with the bone folder to adhere (Figure 4). Take your traced template and place it right side down on your work surface. Retrace the features using a pencil. Turn the tracing right side up and align it with the face and neck. Using a ballpoint pen, retrace the features, pressing firmly, to transfer the outline to the front of your card (Figure 5). Attach the remaining features, using the outline you just made to guide placement (Figure 6). Consider embellishing with other details, such as cheeks, earrings, hats, scarves, or freckles.

See pages 134–136 for instructions on making and lining the envelope.

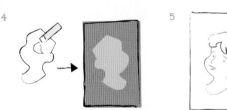

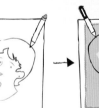

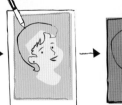

variations:

Pattern portrait. Create a patterned background for your portrait to add depth to the card: Choose a patterned text-weight paper and trim it to a slightly larger size than your folded card. Apply glue to the back of your selected paper and lay it facedown on your work surface. Place the front of the folded card onto your paper (keeping the card folded), and press firmly to adhere. Next, take the right-hand side of your patterned paper and fold it over the back of your folded card; smooth out any air bubbles. Unfold the card and trim excess. Also consider choosing unexpected (but flattering!) patterns for your friend's hair or other features.

Doodle details. Add details to your portrait using a regular or colored pen. Draw a decorative collar, or add details that are too fine to cut out of paper.

Pet portrait. Use the same technique to create a portrait of your friend's dog, cat, hamster, or parakeet. Use it as an everyday card, a thank you note for pet-sitting, or as a thoughtful pet sympathy note.

Bride and groom. Apply the technique to a photo of your favorite couple and present it to them on their wedding day. It will make a great addition to their wedding scrapbook!

Name:

La Familia Green

(Mollie Green)

Location: Chicago, Illinois

How did you get into crafting and/or card making? A couple of years after receiving a BFA in printmaking from the School of the Art Institute of Chicago, I found myself working in a stationery store. Inspired by the independent card designers we carried, I started making cards for the store, and La Familia Green was born.

What is your favorite medium? Turning nothing into something: reusing supermarket flyers, discarded magazines, scraps of origami paper, et cetera.

What is the most memorable card you've ever received (or sent)? The first postcard my now-husband sent me before we even started dating—it's from Duluth, Minnesota.

What is your favorite card-sending occasion? Valentine's Day.

What is the one crafting tool you can't live without? Monoadhesive.

What things most inspire your work? My grandmother's house, which is full of folk art from Poland and Peru; ceramics from France and Portugal; handkerchiefs from Madeira; vintage embroidered linens; Chanel handbags; and lots of drawings, paintings, and photos.

What Web site is your favorite source of inspiration? http://printpattern.blogspot.com.

Where can we find you on the Web? www.lafamiliagreen.com.

VIR
GO
words
power.
to know where you stand.
July 22-Aug. 22): You're on the
of big changes in your personal
Get ready for an exciting two weeks.
SAGITTARIUS

daily horoscope birthday card [BASIC]

you'll need

Pencil

Ruler

Card stock or chipboard (about 5 x 8")
for making your stencil

Clear packing tape or Scotch tape

Utility knife

Cutting mat, or a magazine

Drafting tape

6 to 8 pieces of newspaper

Blank folded card (any size—choose a
larger size for longer words)

Gouache or watercolors in 3 to 4 colors

Cup of water

Paint tray or plate

Paintbrush

Horoscope, cut out of a newspaper or
magazine (no more than 3" wide)

Decorative tape or glue stick

You are a most gracious and cherished friend and can expect many good things. Wherever you go today, good times will follow. There is therefore no better day for you to delight a favorite pal with a special gift. Channel your creative energy into making a fabulous die-cut horoscope card filled with humorous thoughts and insights. You will be showered with praise and affection.

how to:

1 Draw the design for your stencil.
Start with a blank folded card (Figure 1). Using a pencil and ruler, mark a rectangle the size of your card's front panel on the card stock you are using to make your stencil (Figure 2). Draw the name of the chosen astrological sign within this rectangle—the letters can run off the edge of the rectangle a bit (Figure 3). Don't worry about drawing perfect letters, a somewhat naive look is what you are going for.

2 Make the stencil
Once you are satisfied with your design, tape over it with clear packing tape to waterproof the stencil. Cut out the letters using a utility knife (Figure 4). We suggest cutting freehand for a handmade look, but you can also use a ruler. For letters that have negative space, such as *P* or *O*, either leave the negative space solid, or keep the loose piece (e.g. the inside of the *O*) and hold it firmly in place with one finger as you paint over the stencil.

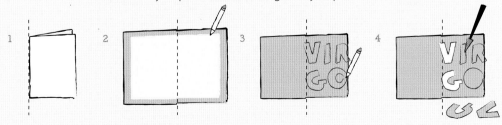

27

Birthday	Star Sign
March 21–April 19	Aries
April 20–May 20	Taurus
May 21–June 20	Gemini
June 21–July 22	Cancer
July 23–August 22	Leo
August 23–September 22	Virgo
September 23–October 22	Libra
October 23–November 21	Scorpio
November 22–December 21	Sagittarius
December 22–January 19	Capricorn
January 20–February 18	Aquarius
February 19–March 20	Pisces

3 Position the stencil on your card.

Using drafting tape, tape several sheets of newspaper down to your work surface. Unfold the blank card and tape the stencil to the front, placing it exactly where you want the image to appear (Figure 5) (in our example, the letters run over to the back of the card). Be sure to test that the tape will not tear the card stock when you peel it off. If necessary, stick and unstick it to a piece of fabric a few times to lessen the tack. Tape the top, bottom, and right-hand side of the card to your work surface.

4 Paint the card.

Mix the gouache or watercolors with enough water to create a rich but transparent wash. (We recommend testing your colors on a piece of scrap paper first.) Paint over each letter in your stencil (Figure 6). Remove the stencil and let the card dry for 30 minutes, or until it is dry to the touch.

5 Cut out the horoscope window.

Choose an amusing or meaningful line(s) from the horoscope. Measure its length and height with a ruler. Using a pencil, mark a corresponding rectangle on the front of the card. This will be your horoscope window, which should be placed so that the entire horoscope will fit inside the card and one line can be read through the window. Cut out the window with a utility knife (Figure 7).

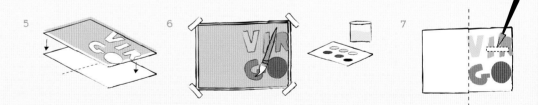

6 Add the horoscope.

Affix two pieces of decorative tape along the right and left sides of the horoscope, or dab glue onto the back (Figure 8). Hold the horoscope against the inside of the front of your card (the sticky side should be facing away from the front of the card), and position it so that the line of text you want to highlight appears in the window (Figure 9). Holding the horoscope in place with one finger, carefully close the card so that the horoscope adheres to the inside of the card (Figure 10). Remove your finger and make sure that the horoscope is in the correct position. If it's not positioned correctly, carefully peel it up and try again. Once you are satisfied with the horoscope's placement, smooth it to adhere completely.

variations:

Baby's first horoscope. Cut out the horoscope from your baby's birthday (for multiple announcements, choose a free newspaper, or have friends collect a variety of newspapers for you). Stencil the baby's name or the words *New baby* on the outside of the card. Write or rubber-stamp the baby's vital statistics inside the card.

Fortune-cookie card. Instead of a horoscope, use the fortune from a Chinese fortune cookie. Select a greeting for the front of the card that matches the fortune—in our example, we use the word *Friend* and a fortune that reads, *You are strongly tuned to those around you.* Sometimes these simple fortunes are unexpectedly profound, so the right one can make a good sympathy card, too.

Star alignment. For a fabulous valentine, anniversary, or wedding card, select a compatibility horoscope (from a newspaper, magazine, or Web site) that represents the signs of the couple, for example "Capricorn and Taurus." Write an appropriate greeting on the front of the card, such as *Perfect match, Soul mate,* or *Love.*

Name:

Egg Press

(Kara Yanagawa and Tess Darrow)

Location: Portland, Oregon

How did you get into crafting and/or card making?
Kara: Kindergarten class! Our teacher was really into hands-on crafts—I loved it.
Tess: I don't remember—it's been a while.

What is your favorite medium?
Kara: I love fabric and paper.
Tess: Letterpress!

What is the most memorable card you've ever received (or sent)?
Kara: I made a birthday card for my friend Norm one year. It was a flat panel card, to which I attached bendy straws—a string through the straws and holes in the card, tied at the back—to make a "curtain rod," miniature curtains, and a painting of puppets with a happy birthday message.
Tess: My son Rye's first birthday invitation. The card had the words *Rye toast!* stitched onto a small piece of rye toast. His birthday is on New Year's Eve, so the message related both to a celebratory toast and his name!

What is your favorite card-sending occasion?
Kara: Everyday/thinking of you.
Tess: Birthdays.

What is the one crafting tool you can't live without?
Kara: My sewing machine.
Tess: Knitting needles.

What things most inspire your work?
Kara: The people for whom I make the work.
Tess: Old books, collaborating with friends.

What Web site is your favorite source of inspiration?
Kara: Too hard to answer!
Tess: www.purlsoho.com and www.shescrafty.com.

Where can we find you on the Web?
www.eggpress.com.

Kate Sutton

pop-up birdie hello
MODERATE

you'll need

Gouache or acrylic paints

Brush

3³/₄ x 9¹/₄" folded card

Ruler

Utility knife

Cutting mat, or a magazine

Bone folder

Black pen

8¹/₂ x 11" sheet of text-weight paper to match your card

Glue stick

4¹/₈ x 9¹/₂" envelope (we suggest using a no. 10 end-opening envelope; see Special Materials by Project, page 140)

This peppy pop-up card makes us want to burst into song! Outside, a little chickadee sleeps, letting out nary a peep about the gregarious warblers inside. The element of surprise makes this a perfect celebratory card, as well as a cheerful way to just say *Hello*.

how to:

1 Paint the birds.

Paint three spots centered along the fold line of your card (Figure 1). Distribute the spots according to the height you'd like your birds to be (more or less evenly if you'd like them to be about the same size, unevenly if you'd like some of your birds to be squat and others to be gangly and tall). Our bird bodies are about 1¹/₄" in diameter.

2 Cut the birds' beaks.

Cut three horizontal slits roughly 1" long (or in proportion to the size of your birds), one across the center of each spot, each extending an even amount on either side of the fold of your card (Figure 2).

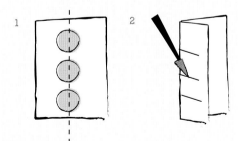

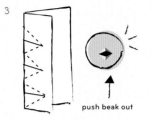

3

push beak out

3 Fold the birds' beaks, and draw on details.

Fold your card, keeping the bird-body spots on the inside. Align your ruler from a point on the fold $1/4$" ($1/2$" for larger birds) above the first slit diagonally to the end of the slit. Score this line using your bone folder. Keeping the card folded, align your ruler from a point on the fold $1/4$" below the first slit diagonally to the end of the slit. Score this line using your bone folder. Turn your card over and repeat on the other side of the slit. Repeat this process for the top and bottom and front and back of each slit. The result should be a diamond shape around each slit. Open your card up and push the slits from the outside of the card toward you, popping the paper out to create your birds' beaks (Figure 3). Draw wings, eyes, and legs onto each bird using your black pen.

4 Adhere the front of your card.

Lay your matching text-weight paper, wrong side up, on your work surface (this will be the front of your card, covering the back side of the birds' beaks). Apply glue to the right and left edges of the back of your birdie card. Center the birdie card on the text-weight paper and smooth to adhere (Figure 4). Carefully fold the card and paper together, smoothing out any air bubbles. Unfold the card, and trim any excess card stock along the edges, using your utility knife, ruler, and cutting mat.

5 Embellish the front of the card.

Paint another bird on the front of your card (Figure 5).

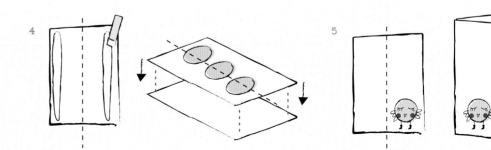

variations:

Open wide! For added dimension, add color to the inside of the birds' beaks by sandwiching a piece of red or pink paper between the front and back of the card. Before Step 4, cut a strip of paper approximately $1/4$" shorter than the length of your card and 1" wider than the cuts you made for the birds' beaks. Fold this strip of paper in half lengthwise, and apply glue to the right and left edges on the right side. Align the fold in the paper with the card fold, covering the back side of all the birds' beaks. Press firmly along the edges of the paper to adhere. Continue to Step 4.

Decorate your envelope. Using your black pen, doodle hints as to what is inside—an amusing worm, a birdcage, a nest with some eggs (say, for a baby announcement)—or paint another bird, perhaps peeping up from the bottom of the envelope.

Playful paper. To make the card even more exuberant, consider using a piece of text-weight paper in a playful color or pattern for the outside of your card.

Christmas carolers. Add Santa hats to each of the birdies by painting triangles on their heads using red gouache. Glue down cotton trim for extra flair, or add details using white gouache or a gel pen.

Repeating refrain. Have lots to crow about? Add another chorus (or two!) of birdies. Start with a piece of card stock that is three (or more!) times as wide as your envelope, less $1/4$" on all sides. Fold it in thirds so that the two flaps close over the middle panel. Follow the original instructions to make each column of birds and beaks.

Name:

Kate Sutton

Location: Liverpool, United Kingdom

How did you get into crafting and/or card making? It's just something I've done since I was little.

What is your favorite medium? Simple pen and paper! I love drawing. Oh, and a bit of collage is always fun!

What is the most memorable card you've ever received (or sent)? My friend bought me a screen print by one of my favorite artists and turned it into a card.

What is your favorite card-sending occasion? When there's no occasion at all. It's nice just to send someone a card in the post every now and again.

What is the one crafting tool you can't live without? Pens.

What things most inspire your work? Nature is a huge inspiration; I never get bored of drawing trees and birds. Also, I love the repeat patterns found in old fabrics and vintage wallpaper. Artists that inspire me include Tove Jansson, Maurice Sendak, and Boris Hoppek, to name a few.

What Web site is your favorite source of inspiration? www.cutxpaste.com.

Where can we find you on the Web? www.katesutton.co.uk.

wood you be mine? valentine   ADVANCED

you'll need

2 wood or metal picture frames (5 x 7" or larger)

2 pieces of sheer nylon or polyester curtain material, each at least 2" larger on all sides than the frames you selected

Staple gun (if working with wood frames) or duct tape (if working with metal frames)

Big Heart and Bitty Heart templates

Pencil

Paintbrush or glue brush

PVA, Mod Podge, or other nonwater-soluble glue (see Adhesives, page 132)

Work Surface template

Scissors

2"-wide masking tape

6 to 8 sheets of newspaper

8 to 10 pieces of scrap paper (trimmed to 4 x 6")

2 small tubes of block-printing ink in pink, red, or white (see Resources, page 139)

Old credit card

$^3/_{16}$"- or $^1/_8$"-thick balsa wood (trimmed to 4 x 6") (see Special Materials by project, page 140) *(Note: Do **not** use craft basswood.)*

Rubber-stamp alphabet kit

Ink pad

Make this witty, graphic valentine with a simple silk-screen technique that uses basic household items. The spare combination of hearts, woodshop materials, and humor makes this card perfect for guys or girls. Also, silk screen is a great technique to learn, as it simplifies making multiples (think party invitations and holiday cards).

how to:

1   Prepare the frames.
Strip everything out of the picture frames—backing, photo of your ex, mat, and glass—so you're left with an empty frame (Figure 1).

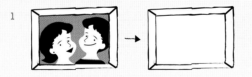

2   Make the screens.
Stretch one piece of the curtain material over the front of one frame as tightly as possible. Secure it on all sides of the frame with a staple gun (for wooden frames) or duct tape (for metal frames). Attach the fabric to the top and bottom of the frame first and then the sides. Pull the fabric as evenly as you can; you'll be able to see and feel the ripples in the fabric when it is uneven (Figure 2). This is Screen 1. Repeat for the second frame. This is Screen 2.

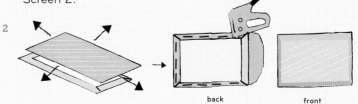

back   front

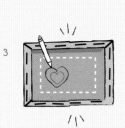

3 Trace the heart templates onto Screen 1.

Placing the frame fabric side down, trace the Big Heart template directly onto the stretched fabric of Screen 1 with a pencil. If you make a mistake, lightly erase your marks or cross them out with hash marks and redraw. Be sure to trace the rectangular dotted line, which indicates the edges of the card, as well as any artwork that extends beyond the dotted line (Figure 3) (the templates provided with this project "bleed" off the edge of the card, so the silk-screened area is larger than the card). Turn the frame over so the fabric side is facing up and you can see your pencil drawing through the fabric.

4 Apply glue to Screen 1.

With the frame fabric side up, use a paintbrush to apply a thin, even coat of Mod Podge to the areas outside of the design you have traced on your screen; apply until these areas are completely covered (Figure 4). The goal is to block out all the areas you do not want to print, leaving the areas you do want to print uncoated so the ink will be able to pass through the pores in the fabric. Set the screen aside for 30 minutes to dry. After the layer is mostly dry, check the screen for pinholes by holding it up to a light source. Apply another layer of Mod Podge to any pinholes. Set the screen aside again, this time for at least 2 hours, or until the glue is completely dry.

5 Make Screen 2.

While you are waiting for the first screen to dry, repeat Steps 3 and 4 with the second screen, this time using the Bitty Heart template.

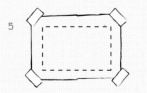

6 Prepare your work surface.

Trace and cut out the Work Surface template. Tape the newspaper to your work surface, covering a large work area. Tape the template down to the newspaper with masking tape (Figure 5).

7 Set up Screen 1.

Turn Screen 1 fabric side down and position it over the Work Surface template, lining up the dotted registration guide with the card outline you marked on your screen (Figure 6). Using masking tape, tape Screen 1 into place along the top edge of the frame only, creating a "hinge" that will allow the frame to flip up while staying in place. Flip Screen 1 up, and position a piece of scrap paper in the center of the Work Surface template (Figure 7). Lower Screen 1 into place over the paper.

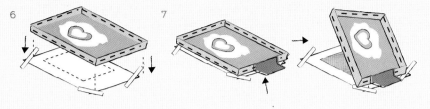

8 Print Screen 1.

Squeeze a line of the lighter colored printing ink along the left edge of the screen (Figure 8). It should be about the same height as the artwork. Holding the frame firmly in place, take your credit card and drag the ink from the left edge all the way across the design area (Figure 9). Don't push too hard; the holes in the fabric are probably pretty large, so it will not take much to get the ink to pass through. Carefully raise the frame to the "up" position and view the print. Make a few test prints on scrap paper to get a feel for how much ink you'll need; you may need to make more than one pass over the ink with your credit card. Once you are happy with the quality of the print, position your balsa-wood card in the center of the Work Surface template and make a print on it (Figure 10). Set the card aside for 30 minutes or until the ink is completely dry to the touch. Repeat as necessary if you are making multiples.

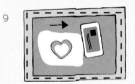 

9 Print Screen 2. and add your message.

Repeat the above steps with Screen 2, using the darker color ink. If you want to reuse either image at a later date, rinse the screens with water to remove the ink once you've finished printing. Using your rubber-stamp alphabet kit, stamp your message onto the card.

Name:

Two Trick Pony

(Laurie Mee and Carrie Siegel, aka "the ponies")

Location: Boston, Massachusetts

How did you get into crafting and/or card making? Having grown up crafting with our moms, we were destined for a lifetime of creativity. After years of art school and a decade of design-oriented jobs, we banded together to create small works of art in the form of greeting cards.

What is your favorite medium? Screen printing, gelatin printing, block printing, and Gocco.

What is the most memorable card you've ever received (or sent)?
Carrie: A mixed-media collage on two vintage switch-plate covers sent to my husband for our first Valentine's Day.
Laurie: A retro 1960s Easter bunny card from my mom.

What is your favorite card-sending occasion? Valentine's Day!

What is the one crafting tool you can't live without? Bone folder—the unsung hero of paper crafts.

What things most inspire your work? Vintage wallpaper and textiles, particularly from the 1950s through the 1970s. We love trolling flea markets and yard sales for old curtains, hankies, pillowcases, et cetera!

What Web site is your favorite source of inspiration? www.secondhandrose.com, www.marimekko.com, www.reprodepot.com, and http://ragandbone.com/blogger.

Where can we find you on the Web? www.twotrickpony.com.

variations:

Print and pattern. Make your own template for a third screen by drawing freehand or tracing clip art (see Trace and Transfer, page 137) or fabric patterns (perhaps add a third heart or print a background pinstripe, polka dot, or brocade pattern). Print the third screen following the original instructions above. To achieve a rich, layered effect with your colors, mix a dab of block-printing ink extender with your ink—this will make the ink more transparent, allowing underlying colors to show through (see Resources, page 139).

Wood you come to dinner? Make this into a stylish dinner party invitation by exchanging the hearts for a graphic place setting. Make the dinner plate on Screen 1: using a compass, draw a circle approximately 2" in diameter and a second, smaller circle within it. Draw a knife and fork (and/or spoon) on Screen 2: trace clip art (see Clip-Art Transfer, page 134), or draw the utensils freehand. Use your rubber-stamp alphabet kit to print the event's details on the back of the card.

MikWright
cocktail hour photo card BASIC

you'll need

Amusing, quite possibly embarrassing photos of family members or friends (see page 40 for tips on choosing your photos)

Utility knife or scissors

Ruler

Cutting mat, or a magazine

Color-copier or scanner and ink-jet printer (optional)

Typewriter, rubber-stamp alphabet kit, or pen

1 to 2 pieces of scrap paper

Glue gun or glue stick

4¼ x 6¼" folded card

Bone folder (optional)

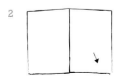

Looking for creative card-making inspiration? Look no further than those dusty old photo albums in Grandma's attic. That circa-1965 shot of Aunt Cheryl looking ever-the-comely-fashionista in a plaid pants suit is crying out for an audience (and some clever commentary)! These ultrapersonal cards are ideal for birthdays, weddings, or anniversaries—actually, any occasion marking the incredibly embarrassing passage of time.

how to:

1 Find a vintage photograph.

Select an appropriately amusing photograph (see "Things to look for . . . " on page 40 for tips on spotting the perfect photo). Trim the photo so it fits on the card while also drawing the focus to your subject's out-of-control flares, enormous hamster-figurine collection, or outstanding dance moves (Figure 1). (Consider color-copying or scanning and printing your photo onto photo paper to preserve the priceless original. To scan and print the photo: Place it facedown on your scanner bed and close the cover, then follow your software's instructions for scanning. Adjust the size, and print on photo paper—available at most office-supply stores—using a color ink-jet printer.)

2 Write a caption.

Come up with a wry one-liner. Here's where a cocktail may come in handy (or see "Things to look for . . . " on page 40 for some help). Type your pithy observation inside the card (Figure 2). We suggest that you practice text placement on a piece of scrap paper first. You can always render your lettering using a rubber-stamp alphabet kit or a pen, should a typewriter be in short supply.

Name:

MikWright

(Tim Mikkelsen and Phyllis Wright-Herman)

Location: Charlotte, North Carolina

How did you get into crafting and/or card making? One night, while drinking and perusing old family photos, it dawned on us: we could take our champagne-induced humor on the road with cards.

What is your favorite medium? Vintage family photos.

What is the most memorable card you've ever received (or sent)? Phyllis received a basic thank you card from a past coworker, noting that he had forged a relationship with his dying brother via Mik-Wright cards.

What is your favorite card-sending occasion? Nonoccasion—or all-occasion—cards. Cards sent at nontraditional times often mean more than the obligatory holiday card.

What is the one crafting tool you can't live without? A hot-glue gun.

What things most inspire your work? Seriously wicked, tongued insults. We tone them down, throw a twist on them, and relax with a cocktail.

What Web site is your favorite source of inspiration? www.somelikeitscott.com.

Where can we find you on the Web? www.mikwright.com.

3 Attach the photograph to the front of the card.

Apply glue to the back of your photo, and center the photo on the front of your card, smoothing it with the bone folder or pressing firmly to adhere (Figure 3).

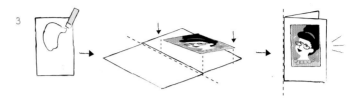

Things to look for when hunting for old photos that will make great cards:

- Friends or relatives in loudly colored polyester
- Big hair, sprayed hard
- Bad Halloween costumes (Uncle Roy as a leprechaun; Grandma Jenkins as a go-go dancer)
- 1970s prom pictures
- Elementary school pictures
- Friends or relatives caught going through ugly duckling phases (Headgear, glasses, AND a back brace? Have mercy!)
- Questionable behavior of any kind

It's true, not everyone came out the other side of adolescence with a biting sense of humor. If you're just a naturally nice person, get warmed up with these funny one-liners (courtesy of MikWright), and find suitable photos to match:

- *She was nothing but a man-chasing boozehound. Why can't you be more like her? Happy birthday.*
- *It's sort of the one I wanted. But heck, I can always re-gift it. Happy holidays.*
- *Hence the age-old question: Which came first . . . polyester or peroxide?*
- *Now remember, kids . . . No running, no diving, and no salt on my margaritas!*

now why did i come into the kitchen?
oh yeah, to fart.

happy birthday.

you'll need

Utility knife

Ruler

Cutting mat, or a magazine

3 sheets of double-sided adhesive film or permanent spray adhesive

Dark- or bright-colored card stock (at least 5 x 7")

Light-colored card stock (at least 5 x 7")

Pencil

2 paper doilies (see Special Materials by Project, page 140)

Scissors

Corner rounder, or a glass to use as a guide for rounding corners (optional)

4 to 6 sheets of newspaper

Envelope

3 pieces of drafting tape

Can of spray paint

Transform patterned paper doilies into elegant, graphic notes. Cut out a favorite section of doily (slightly off-center for dynamic composition), and paste it against a colorful background. Then, use your doily as a stencil to create a delicate pattern on your envelope. (Use white spray paint or primer to create the delectable look of confectioners' sugar!) Make multiples—paper doilies cost pennies— for personal correspondence, save the dates, wedding invitations, or valentines!

how to:

1 Glue your cards together.

Using a utility knife and ruler, cut two sheets of adhesive film that are slightly larger than your card stock (Figure 1). Laying the first piece of film on your work surface, peel off one side of the sticker backing (reserve the second sheet for Step 2). Place your dark card stock wrong side down onto the film. Smooth to adhere. Lay your light card stock wrong side up on your work surface. Peel the remaining sticker backing from the dark card stock. Center the sticky side of the dark card stock on the light-colored card stock. Smooth to adhere. With a pencil and ruler, mark out the finished size of the card. Trim off the excess card stock and adhesive film using your utility knife.

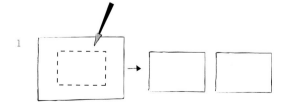

2   Adhere the doily.

Position the first doily on the dark side of your card, aligning it so that the portion you want to use is on the card (Figure 2). With a pencil, lightly mark the edges of the card on your doily (Figure 3) and trim it down with a utility knife. Apply the second sheet of adhesive film to the wrong side of the doily and adhere to the dark side of your card (Figure 4). If desired, round the corners of the card using a corner rounder, or the round edge of a small jar or glass, and your utility knife.

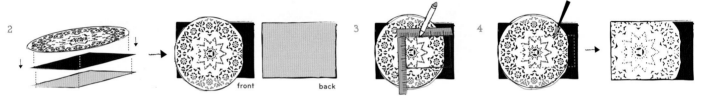

3   Decorate the envelope.

Make sure your work area is well ventilated. Lay down newspaper to protect your work surface. Place your open envelope flap-down on your work surface. Position the doily on top of your envelope, covering the majority of the envelope, and tape it down to your work surface on all sides with drafting tape (Figure 5). Holding the spray paint about 18" away from the envelope, spray a light, even coating over the entire thing (Figure 6). If you are making more than one envelope, carefully lift up the tape on one side of your doily (leaving the tape on the other sides), and remove the envelope. Set it aside to dry, and repeat the process with the rest of your envelopes.

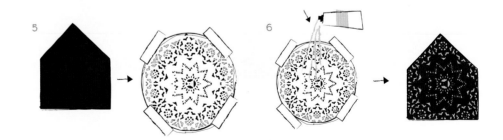

variations:

While these cards are shown as simple blank notes, they can be used for virtually any occasion. Experiment with different doily patterns; those shown here are vintage doilies found at a local flea market, but party supply stores sell a variety of patterns that work just as well (see Special Materials by Project, page 140).

Personal stationery. Create a set of exquisite, personalized correspondence cards. Make multiple cards, perhaps using a variety of doily patterns. Rubber-stamp your initials on the reverse of the card, and consider getting a custom rubber stamp made for your return address (see Resources, page 139).

Save the date or wedding invitation. Use these cards to invite guests to a romantic wedding. Choose colors to match your wedding palette and style (for example, black and ecru for a formal event; red and white for an outdoor summer wedding). Print the event details on the light-colored card stock. If you like, use the same technique to create program covers, menus, seating cards, and table number cards, and consider making pretty paper napkin-rings out of strips cut from the doilies.

Vintage valentine. Use a heart-shaped doily to make a valentine for your sweetheart, choosing red, pink, and ecru or white for the card-stock layers.

Name:

Hello!Lucky

(Eunice Moyle and Sabrina Moyle)

Location: San Francisco, California, and London, United Kingdom

How did you get into crafting and/or card making? Our mom is a crafting queen—she literally has a degree in Home Ec!—and our dad is a self-taught printer, fiddler, and pie maker, so we grew up making everything from scratch. When we fell in love with letterpress, cards seemed like a natural fit—so useful, simple, and satisfying to make!

What is the most memorable card you've ever received (or sent)? A pop-up valentine that we made with the help our friend Anthony Tarantino: It was a gorilla that pounded its chest when you pulled a tab. The card read: *My heart beats for you!*

What is your favorite card-sending occasion? Valentine's Day! We just love all the funny puns and one-liners it elicits, like *Let's be frank*—picture of a hot dog—*You're my Valentine!*

What is the one crafting tool you can't live without? Utility knife with lots of fresh blades and a black Stylist felt-tip pen—the best felt-tip pen on the planet!

What things most inspire your work? Flea markets, vintage wallpapers and fabrics—especially Osborne & Little and Liberty of London—and things we discover when we travel, which is as often as possible!

What Web site is your favorite source of inspiration? www.anthropologie.com and www.dominomag.com.

Where can we find you on the Web? www.hellolucky.com.

Sarah L. M. Adler

magical birthday banner ADVANCED

you'll need

Pencil (2B or softer)

Tracing paper

Blank Oval, Playing Card Ovals, Rabbit, and Rabbit Accoutrements templates

One 8 1/2 x 11" piece of cardboard (or mat board)

Scissors

Five 8 1/2 x 11" sheets each of red, black, and white text-weight paper

Utility knife

Glue stick

2" alphabet stencils (see Resources, page 139)

8 1/2 x 11" manila file folder

Black and red permanent markers and white gel pen (optional)

Craft glue

Three 2-oz jars of red, white, and black glitter

5 feet of 1"-wide red satin ribbon, plus 5" of 1"-wide ribbon for the hat band bow

Two 3 1/2" x 3 1/2" oval, unfinished, papier mâché boxes (see Special Materials by Project, page 140)

Black gaffer tape (see Resources, page 139)

4-oz tube black acrylic or tempera paint

Paintbrush

Cutting mat, or a magazine

1/4 yard of red satin fabric

Ruler

Packaged in a deceptively dainty little box shaped like a top hat, this magical birthday banner reveals itself one sparkling letter and mischievous rabbit at a time. Once the bedecked satin ribbon is unfurled, it can be strung up to decorate a room for a party!

how to:

1   Make the ovals.

Trace and transfer the Blank Oval template provided onto cardboard to create a reusable stencil (see Trace and Transfer, page 138). Cut out the oval shape using scissors (Figure 1). Trace the oval 25 times onto a combination of black, red, and white papers, making one or two extras just in case. Cut out each oval (Figure 2). These will be used for the alphabet letters.

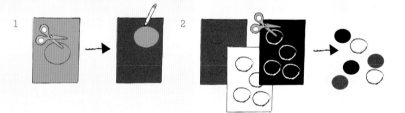

Trace and transfer the Playing Card Ovals templates onto a combination of black, red, and white papers, tracing each shape two to three times for a total of nine ovals and making one or two extras just in case. Cut out each of the ovals with scissors.

2   Make the rabbits and letters.

Trace and transfer the four Rabbit templates onto a combination of black and white papers, tracing each shape two to three times for a total of 11 rabbit templates. Trace and transfer the Accoutrements (hat, flag, kazoo, candle) you would like to use with your rabbits onto a combination of papers. Cut out the shapes with a utility knife. Using a glue stick, glue the rabbits and their accessories to a combination of red, white, and black ovals (Figure 3). Using the alphabet stencils, trace the letters for *Happy Birthday* onto the blank oval cutouts, one letter for each oval (Figure 4).

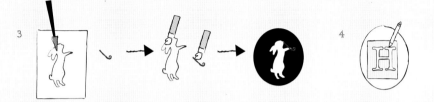

3 Glitter the letters.

Open the file folder and lay it flat on your work surface. Place the first letter on top of the file folder (Figure 5). (Optional: Fill in the letter with a permanent marker or gel pen that matches the glitter color you plan to use; this will give the letter a more opaque look.) Fill in the letter with craft glue (Figure 6). Sprinkle glitter to completely cover the glue (Figure 7). To remove the excess, tap the oval over the center of the file folder. Fold the file folder in half and return the excess glitter to its container (Figure 8). Repeat for the remaining alphabet letters.

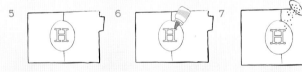

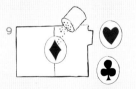

4 Make the playing card symbols.

Repeat Step 3, this time with the playing card symbols, glittering each club, diamond, heart, and spade with the desired colors (Figure 9).

5 Assemble the banner.

Apply glue to the wrong side of one rabbit oval with your glue stick. Lay the oval on your work surface wrong side up, and position your ribbon on the oval so that it runs through the narrow center and leaves a 5" tail on one side, making sure the rabbit is facing away from the tail. Apply glue to the wrong side of a second rabbit oval (Figure 10). Making sure the rabbit also faces away from the short end of the ribbon, place the rabbit oval right side up on top of the first oval, sandwiching the ribbon between them (Figure 11). Repeat for each letter, alternating between rabbits and playing card symbols for the backs of the letters, spelling out *Happy Birthday*, and leaving about 1" of ribbon between each letter. The left side of each letter should face toward the tail so that the banner reads left-to-right, like a garland. Use a rabbit oval between the words *Happy* and *Birthday*. (If you want your banner to hang vertically, rotate the letters 90 degrees counterclockwise so they can be read top-to-bottom when pulled from the box.) End the banner with another rabbit oval. You should have about 3" of ribbon left at the end of your banner. Fold the end of the ribbon in half lengthwise, and trim it with scissors at a 45-degree angle, creating a cut-out V-shape (Figure 12).

6 Make the box into a top hat.

Cut the top off the base of one of the oval-shaped papier mâché boxes and discard the cutout portion, creating an open-ended cylinder (Figure 13). Fit open end of the base of the second papier mâché box on top of the cut box and tape them together using gaffer tape, taping both inside and outside (Figure 14). Using black acrylic paint, paint the outside of the box and let dry. Once dry, cover all but the bottom 1/2" of the sides with black glitter, one section at a time, following the instructions in Step 3 (the

leave 1/2"

15   ¹/₂"

nonglittered portion will be the portion that fits into the base of the hat).
Lay one of the remaining box lids on top of the cardboard, and trace the
oval shape. (The second lid can be discarded.) Draw another oval, ¹/₂"
larger on all sides, around the lid shape. Cut out the board along the larger
oval line using a utility knife (Figure 15). (This shape will be the brim of the
top hat.) Using the gaffer tape, attach the remaining box lid upside-down
to the brim. Paint the outside of the lid and brim black and let dry. Once
dry, cover the top and bottom of the brim with black glitter (Figure 16).
(Leave the sides of the box attached to the brim unglittered.) Cut a length
of red satin fabric, large enough to line the inside of the top hat. Apply
craft glue to the back of the satin and press it along the inside wall of the
box/hat (Figure 17).

16

17

7   Make a red hatband.

Cut a length of red satin fabric that is double the depth of your lid in width
and long enough to cover the entire circumference of the lid. Apply craft
glue to the wrong side of the fabric and affix it lengthwise along the rim,
where it meets the base (Figure 18). Fold the satin over the edge of the rim,
affixing the other half to the inside of the rim.

18   fold over

8   Make a bow for your hatband.

Cut a 3" length of ribbon, and then cut it in half lengthwise. Take one of the
halves, fold in the ends to meet in the middle, and tack it into place with craft
glue, creating a bow shape (Figure 19). Trim the other ribbon-half to 2¹/₂" long.
Fold each end of the ribbon in half lengthwise, and trim with scissors at a
45-degree angle, creating a cutout V-shape. Center this piece along the back
of your bow so that each V-shape peeks out from behind either side of the bow,
and tack it into place using craft glue. Cut a piece of ribbon ¹/₂" wide and 1¹/₄"
long. Wrap this piece around the middle of your bow and glue the ends in place.

19

9 Affix the banner to the inside of the base of your top hat.

Take a playing card oval and, using a utility knife and ruler, cut a slit in the center of the oval that is slightly wider than your ribbon (Figure 20). Slide about 1" of the tail at the beginning of your banner through the slit, from the right side through to the wrong side, feeding it so that the text on the banner faces the same way as the right side of the playing card oval (Figure 21). Apply glue to the side of the ribbon facing the wrong side of the playing card oval, and smooth to adhere. Apply glue to the wrong side of the playing card oval, and carefully position and adhere it to the inside of the base of your top hat (Figure 22).

10 Decorate the box, and assemble the card.

Apply glue to one side of a rabbit oval, and affix it to the top of the hat (Figure 23). Lay the top of the hat upside down. Accordion-fold the banner, starting with the loose end, and tuck it one section at a time into the upturned hat until you reach the base/brim (Figure 24). Tuck the brim of the hat, upside down, into the upturned top. Flip the hat over (Figure 24).

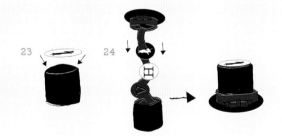

Name:

Sarah L. M. Adler

Location: San Francisco, California

How did you get into crafting and/or card making? I remember crafting cards for my grandmothers and parents on rainy afternoons in Oregon when I was about four years old. I spent hours snipping away at brightly hued construction paper and scribbling heartfelt crayon messages.

What is your favorite medium? I love letterpress, screen printing, and Polaroid film.

What is the most memorable card you've ever received (or sent)? A shoe. A friend of mine once sent me a note written on a woman's ecru-colored, circa-1980 pump, with my address on the sole and the postage stamps stuck directly onto the leather. I was amazed that it was even delivered, and at that point, I embarked upon an endless adventure to test the post office's limits.

What is your favorite card-sending occasion? Unbirthdays and the holidays.

What is the one crafting tool you can't live without? An X-Acto knife; Yes! Stik Flat Glue; and double-sided tape.

What things most inspire your work? Old architecture that has fallen into disrepair, ships, ports, barns, ghost towns, train stations, Victorian wallpaper, 1960s textiles, all things nautical, vintage sheet music, vintage LP art, found photographs, and stereo views.

What Web site is your favorite source of inspiration? www.clipart.com.

Where can we find you on the Web? www.heartsandanchors.com.

variations:

Simple banner in a box. Create a pretty round or square box, rather than an oval top hat, that reveals a delightful banner of your own design. Take advantage of the many fabulous typefaces, images, and frames available in clip-art books (see Resources, page 139). Photocopy the patterns, letters, and clip-art images to create the panels of the banner, and embellish using a bit of glitter or colored pens.

Get well soon. Use this card concept to cheer up a friend or brighten a hospital room. Select cheerful imagery, such as a bouquet of flowers, and design the banner and box around an encouraging message.

Music box. Consider adding a music-box mechanism (or musical movement), available at craft specialty stores, to the bottom of the box (see Special Materials by Project, page 140). Following the instructions that come with the music-box mechanism, affix it to the box, and set it to play a jaunty tune when the box is opened.

You Send Me
sparkly thank you bouquet MODERATE

The glitter and tiny seed beads on this dainty card create a dazzling bouquet—a sweet and sophisticated way to say *Thank you* or to celebrate a birthday, mother's day, or wedding. Make the card with iridescent paper for an extra-radiant effect!

you'll need

Ruler or right angle

Pencil

1 sheet of iridescent card stock (at least 5 x 7")

Decorative-edged scissors

1 to 2 pieces of scrap paper

Sparkly Bouquet templates

Assortment of colored pencils and pens (gel pens work especially well)

Rubber-stamp alphabet kit (optional)

Ink pad (optional)

Letter-sized file folder or a piece of newspaper

3 to 4 small jars of glitter in different colors (see Special Materials by Project, page 140)

Craft glue with ultrafine metal tip attachment

Straight pin

5 seed beads

Glue stick or double-sided tape

4$\frac{1}{2}$ x 6$\frac{1}{2}$" folded card

Additional materials for making Stencil 2 (the Tapered Bouquet):

Toothpick

1 to 2 pieces of scrap paper

Awl, or a utility knife

Large embroidery needle

6" length of 1/8" ribbon

Scissors

how to:

1 **Trim the card stock.**
Start with a blank folded card (Figure 1). Using a ruler or right angle, measure and mark a 4$\frac{1}{4}$ x 5$\frac{1}{4}$" rectangle on the card stock. Trim with decorative-edged scissors (Figure 1). It's a good idea to practice cutting some scrap paper first, as it can be tricky to get the decorative corners to match up exactly.

2 **Draw the bouquet.**
Draw a bouquet in pencil on the card stock, using the petal, flower, leaf, stem, and bow shapes from the Sparkly Bouquet template provided (Figure 2). Be sure to leave room for a message, if you want to include one. Once you are happy with your design, retrace or draw your flowers with colored pencils or pens.

thank you

m o m

3 Add a message.

Stamp a message using your rubber-stamp alphabet kit, or hand-letter the message using colored pencils or pens (Figure 3). Let it dry.

4 Glitter the flowers, leaves, and bow.

(Note: Instructions in this step apply to Stencil 1. If you are using Stencil 2, see the Tapered Bouquet *instructions under Variations for information about making the tapered petals.)*

Open the file folder and lay it flat on your work surface. Place the bouquet drawing on top of the file folder. Decide on the glitter colors you will use for each part of the bouquet. Using the craft glue with ultrafine metal tip attachment, trace and fill in the areas that will have the darkest glitter color (Figure 4). Sprinkle the glue with plenty of glitter to get good coverage (the excess can be reused) (Figure 5). To remove the excess, tap the card over the center of the file folder (it works quite well to flick the back of the card with your index finger). Fold the file folder in half, and return the excess glitter to its container (Figure 6). Switch colors. If you find the glitter sticking outside of the lines, nudge it into place using a straight pin. Repeat for each color on your bouquet, working from darkest glitter to lightest, allowing each color to dry for a few minutes before continuing. Fill in the bow using the craft glue with the tip attachment and glitter. Let it dry.

5 Add beads to the centers of the flowers.

Place a drop of glue in the center of a flower. Pick up a seed bead using the tip of a straight pin and place it on its side on the glue dot, holding it gently in place with a finger as you remove the pin (Figure 7). Let it dry.

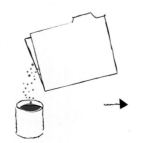

8

6 Mount your bouquet.

Apply glue or double-sided tape to the back of the card stock; center the card stock on the front of your blank card, carefully applying pressure to adhere (Figure 8).

variations:

Tapered Bouquet (Stencil 2). Make a bouquet with pretty tapered flower petals. Follow the original instructions with the following variations:

Before Step 4. Add the tapered petals.

On the stencil, tapers are indicated with a small circle. Squeeze out a dot of craft glue, and pull it into a taper by placing the tip of a toothpick in the center of the dot and dragging it in the direction you'd like your taper to go (Figure 1). Practice a few of these on scrap paper before working them into your project. Let dry until firm to the touch. Follow the instructions in Step 4 to apply glitter to the tapered petals, and then make the dots, stems, and flowers.

5. Add a ribbon.

Use an awl or utility knife to make holes or small slits on either side of the bouquet, approximately midstem (Figure 2). Using a large embroidery needle, thread the ribbon from front to back through one hole or slit, leaving a tail in the front, and then from back to front through the second hole (Figure 3). Tie a knot or bow on the front of the card, and trim the ends at an angle using scissors (Figure 4).

1

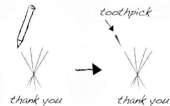

toothpick

thank you → thank you →

2

thank you

3

thank you

4

thank you

56

Mother's Day bouquet. Make the bouquet, and rubber-stamp the word *Mom* on the front of the card. Accompany with a real bouquet of mom's favorite flowers!

Wedding bouquet. To congratulate friends on their marriage, position the bouquet at an angle on the card, so it looks like it has just been tossed.

Save the date bouquet. Make this card assembly line–style: Affix the bouquet to a flat card that is preprinted with your wedding details. Stamp the words *Save the date*, or your wedding date, under the bouquet. If desired, include a second flat card printed with accommodation and travel information, and decorate this card with a sprinkle of glitter flowers. Be sure to mail the pieces in an envelope so that the glitter doesn't get damaged.

Name:

You Send Me

(Jenni Kelly and Karen Leads)

Location: Chattanooga, Tennessee

How did you get into crafting and/or card making? Best friends since eighth grade, one January day in 1998 we decided, "What do we have to lose?" So, we made some cards and brought them to our favorite store in Seattle. The owner bought some, much to our shock and delight!

What is your favorite medium? Glitter!

What is the most memorable card you've ever received (or sent)?
Karen: A handmade card my grandmother, Gudrun, sent me when I was ten.
Jenni: The hand-watercolored birthday cards my mom sends me every year.

What is your favorite card-sending occasion? Our children's birthday party invitations.

What is the one crafting tool you can't live without? Fine-nibbed glue pen.

What things most inspire your work? Everything vintage.

What Web site is your favorite source of inspiration? More than any Web site, we reach for our boxes of vintage ribbons, pins, and other collectibles.

Where can we find you on the Web?
www.yousendme.com and http://shop.yousendme.com.

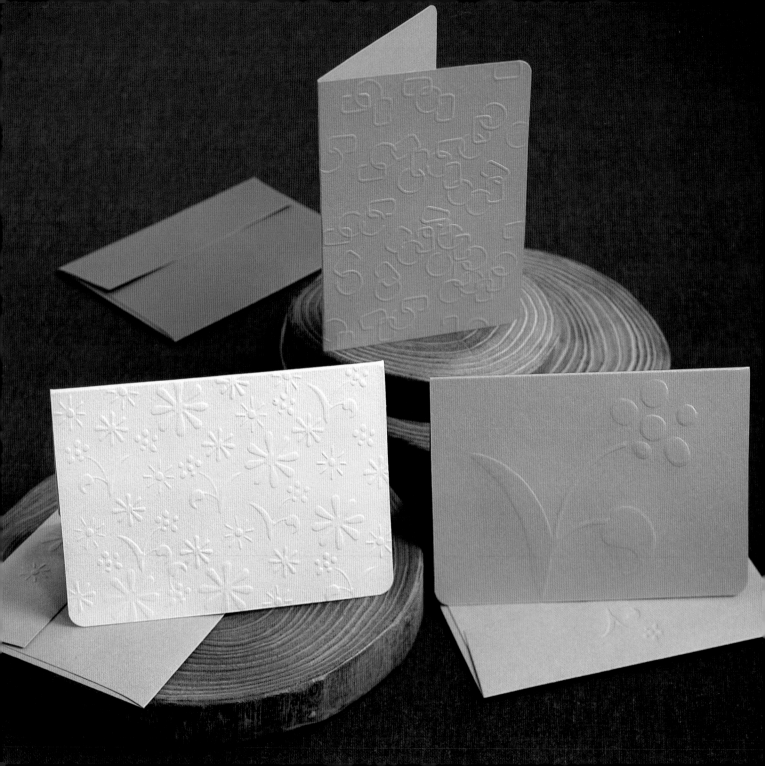

embossed stencil correspondence card `MODERATE`

you'll need

Embossing stencils

Pencil, 2B or softer

8¹/₂ x 11" sheet of tracing paper

Ballpoint pen

8¹/₂ x 11" sheet of card stock

Utility knife, with a fresh blade

Cutting mat, or a magazine

1 blank folded card (any size)

Drafting tape

Light box, or a sunny windowpane

12" sheet of wax paper

Hand-embossing tool (see Special Materials by Project, page 140), or a pointed bone folder

Corner rounder, or a glass to use as a guide for rounding corners (optional)

8¹/₂ x 11" sheet of colored, text-weight paper (optional)

Scissors

Double-sided tape or glue stick (optional)

This lovely project involves using simple stencils to achieve a professional-quality embossed look. The stencil does the work for you, making it easy to achieve a polished result with minimal skill and effort. Apply the pattern to the front and back of the card, as well as the flap of the envelope!

how to:

1   **Make your stencil.**

Trace and transfer one of the Embossed stencils provided onto the sheet of card stock (see Trace and Transfer, page 138). Cut out the stencil using a utility knife (Figure 1).

2   **Position the stencil on your card.**

Using the drafting tape, attach your stencil to the front of a blank folded card exactly where you want the image to appear (Figure 2). (Make sure you test the tape to be sure it won't tear the card stock when you peel it off. If necessary, stick and unstick it to a piece of fabric a few times to lessen the tack.) Place your card facedown on the light box, or tape it facedown on the pane of a sunny window (Figure 3).

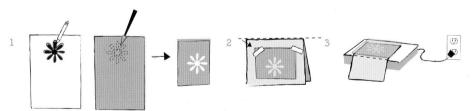

3 Trace the stencil design.

Place a sheet of wax paper on top of your card. (The wax paper allows the embossing tool to glide smoothly over the card, allowing you to press the card along the cut edges of the stencil.) Trace along the inside edge of the stencil's design with the embossing tool, so that the paper is pressed in along the cut edges of your stencil (Figure 4). The center of the traced area will automatically be raised.

If your card stock is too dark to see through using the light box or window, use your fingertip, or any rounded object, to press into the open areas of the stencil. Once you've roughly outlined the embossed area, complete the design using your embossing tool. Alternatively, if you have two of the same stencil, sandwich your card stock between the two stencils and press into the open areas.

4 Create a pattern.

Repeat this process, repositioning your stencil to create an allover pattern (Figure 5). If you'd like, round the corners of the card using a corner rounder or decorative punch.

5 Cut out a liner and affix it to your card (optional).

If you are using a dark-colored paper for your card, a lighter liner might make for a better writing surface. Create this liner by cutting a lighter sheet of text-weight paper 1/8" smaller than your card on all sides. Center the card liner on the inside of your card. Holding the liner in place, fold both the card and the liner, and crease. Lift the front of your card and apply glue or double-sided tape to the back of the liner. Fold the front of your card back down, and smooth to adhere.

6 Emboss the envelope flap.

Following Steps 2–4, repeat a portion of the embossed pattern on the flap of your envelope.

variations:

Creative papers. While metallic card stock gives this project extra flair, many other card stocks work beautifully, including classic white printmaking and watercolor papers. You can also try papers that have interesting textures, such as vellum, plasticlike papers, cork-skin papers, and papers with a velvet or fabriclike finish. The key is to find one that is thick and pliable and with a texture that will bring out the embossed pattern.

Stencil mania! There is a whole world of fabulous ready-made stencils out there, as you will shortly discover. Look for brass stencils, which are sturdy and long-lasting. Some of our favorite stencils feature art nouveau motifs, chinoiserie, or floral patterns. Just pick a paper that matches the theme of your stencil, and you're good to go!

Design your own stencil. Choose your own design for a stencil; we suggest looking at wallpaper or textile-pattern books for ideas. Draw or photocopy your image onto a transparency or tracing paper, and then follow the original instructions to stencil your card.

Name:

Cielo Blu

(Michele Luminato)

Location: Portland, Oregon

How did you get into crafting and/or card making? Making cards as a child.

What is your favorite medium? Silk screen, for vibrancy in color.

What is the most memorable card you've ever received (or sent)? A handmade baby card I sent a friend about seven years ago—it had little jewels on it and was so cute—but I remember being shocked that it was $9.00. I bought it anyway.

What is your favorite card-sending occasion? Birthdays.

What is the one crafting tool you can't live without? X-Acto knife.

What things most inspire your work? Colors in shape.

What Web site is your favorite source of inspiration? http://printpattern.blogspot.com.

Where can we find you on the Web? www.cieloblustudios.com.

Hello!Lucky
silhouette save the date ADVANCED

A save the date is the perfect occasion to exercise your creativity by making a card that is both personal and a lasting memento. This one uses silk-screening, a technique that, while advanced, is well worth learning so that you can make multiples (and perhaps even print your own wedding invitations, cocktail napkins, menus, or favors). By far the most involved part is making the screens, but if you're short on time or patience you can bypass this step by having them made for you by professionals (see Resources, page 139).

you'll need

For the layout:

Photographs of you and your honey in profile (can be two separate photos)

Photocopier

Oval Frame and Floral Pattern templates

8 1/2 x 11" sheet of tracing paper

Pencil

Ruler

Fine-tip black felt pen

Computer with word-processing program

Printer

Standard text-weight paper

Scissors

Glue stick

For the screens:

Scissors

Transparent tape

Three 10 x 14" screen-printing frames with fabric (see Special Materials by Project, page 140)

Mild dishwashing soap

Nylon scrub brush

8-oz bottle photo emulsion (see Special Materials by Project, page 140)

2-oz bottle photo emulsion sensitizer (see Special Materials by Project, page 140)

Squeegee (comes with screen-printing unit)

12 plastic-head pushpins

Desk fan (optional)

Desk lamp

Photoflood (250-watt) lightbulb (see Special Materials by Project, page 140)

10" or 12" disposable aluminum pie tin

10 x 14" piece of black paper

Glass from an 8 x 10" picture frame

Toothbrush

For printing:

10 x 14" standard-grade screen-printing unit (see Special Materials by Project, page 140)

Phillips-head screwdriver

Printmaking paper (trimmed to 4 3/4 x 6 1/2"—enough cards to print the number of save the dates you're planning to send out, plus about 30 percent more for errors and test runs. We used Arturo cover-weight in pale blue; see Special Materials by Project, page 140).

Drafting tape

Empty container for mixing ink

8-oz jar of water-soluble screen-printing ink in white, blue, and black (see Special Materials by Project, page 140)

2 spoons

Squeegee (comes with screen-printing unit)

Sponge

Mild dishwashing soap

Toothbrush

Pencil

Right angle

Utility knife

how to:

PART ONE: LAY OUT YOUR CARD

1 Photocopy the pictures and templates.

Make a black-and-white photocopy of your photos, reducing or enlarging as necessary to fit them into the Oval Frame template provided. In addition, make a photocopy of the Oval Frame and Floral Pattern templates.

2 Draw your silhouettes.

Place a piece of tracing paper over the photocopied photo of yourself and, with a pencil, trace your profile, including neck and shoulders. Lay your tracing over one of the ovals in the Oval Frame template, positioning the drawing so that it fits nicely into the frame. With your pencil, shape the bottom of your traced profile so that it follows the curve of the oval, leaving a $1/16$" gap between the bottom of the profile and the oval frame. Trace over your drawing with a black pen, and fill it in completely (Figure 1). Repeat for the silhouette of your honey.

3 Create your text.

Using a computer word-processing program, type the text for the front and back of your save the date (Figure 2). The layout can be very simple (ours is just centered with the names a bit larger), but a pretty font really makes the design (see Resources, page 139; we used Archive Penman Script). Print your text in black ink on standard text-weight paper.

4 Assemble your design.

Cut out your silhouettes, and apply glue to the wrong sides with a glue stick. Carefully position your silhouettes against the photocopy of the Oval Frame template, aligning the bottoms of the silhouettes with the bottom curve of the oval and leaving $1/16$" in from the inside edge of the ovals. Smooth to adhere. Cut out the text for the front of the card. Apply glue to the wrong side of your text with a glue stick and center it below the two ovals (Figure 3).

PART TWO: MAKE YOUR SCREENS

5 Make your positives.

Take your design, your printout of the text for the back of the card, and your photocopy of the Floral Pattern template to a copy shop. Have two transparencies made of each piece, with the artwork centered on the transparency sheet.

Trim off excess transparency film on one of your Floral Pattern transparencies. Carefully align the trimmed transparency to your second Floral Pattern transparency (untrimmed) and tape them in place using transparent tape. Repeat this process for the remaining two sets of transparencies. Each doubled-up transparency will be used to create a separate screen, resulting in three screens. The Floral Pattern screen will be Screen 1. The front of the card (with silhouettes) will be Screen 2. The back of the card will be Screen 3 (Figure 4).

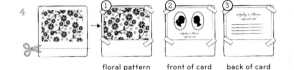

floral pattern   front of card   back of card

6 Prepare your screens.

Using dishwashing soap and a nylon scrub brush, wash both sides of your screens. Let them dry about 30 minutes. Once they're dry, follow the mixing instructions on your containers of photo emulsion and sensitizer. If you're not using these immediately, store them in a cool, dark place (a refrigerator works well).

With Screen 1 front side up (the flat side), pour a bead of photo emulsion across the top of the screen (Figure 5). Starting at this bead of emulsion, drag your squeegee across the screen, spreading the emulsion thinly and evenly (Figure 6). Repeat this process on the back side of the screen, working to achieve an even, continuous coating on both sides of the screen fabric. Be careful to smooth out any extra drips of emulsion. Stick a pushpin into each of the four front corners of the wooden frame, and set the screen, front side down, on the pushpins in an area away from light and heat (Figure 7). A closet, empty drawer, or cardboard box works well. (We used the box our screen-printing unit came in.) Set the screen aside until it is completely dry to the touch—several hours. If you're in a hurry, a fan greatly speeds up the drying time. If you're planning to print more than 300 cards, you should apply a second coat of photo emulsion and let dry. Repeat this process for Screens 2 and 3.

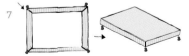

7 Expose your screens.

Remove the shade and existing lightbulb from a desk lamp, and screw in the photoflood lightbulb. Cut an X into the base of an aluminum pie tin, and push the lightbulb through the X, creating a makeshift reflector (Figure 8). Place the sheet of black paper on your work surface. Before removing the sensitized Screen 1 from its dark drying area, make sure you have the glass, Floral Template transparency, and desk lamp at the ready. Remove Screen 1 from its storage space, remove the pushpins, and place it flat side down on your black paper (Figure 9). Place the Floral Pattern transparency on the screen, right side up. Place the piece of glass on top of your transparency for maximum screen contact. Position your desk lamp over the middle of and 12" above your screen. Turn the light on, and let Screen 1 expose for 10 minutes (Figure 10). Repeat for Screens 2 and 3.

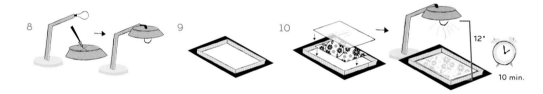

8 Clean the positive areas of the screens.

Once your screen has been fully exposed, blast it with lukewarm water (do not use hot water), moving the screen around to hit all areas. (We used the bathtub with both faucets going full blast.) Firmly brush the screen with a toothbrush on both sides, periodically holding the screen to the light to check your progress. Your artwork won't start opening up until the screen is completely clear of photo emulsion (Figure 11). Be sure to give a thorough washout for a crisp image. Once you are satisfied with the image, rinse the screen one last time with cold water. Set it aside to dry.

PART THREE: PRINT YOUR CARDS

9 Attach Screen 1 to the base of your screen-printing unit.

Assemble the hinges of your screen-printing unit by joining the two halves together with a screwdriver and the hinge pins provided (Figure 12): Position the hinges over the "pilot" holes on the top of Screen 1 and the base, and screw them in place. It is best to mount the side of the hinge with more bearings to the base and the side of the hinge with fewer bearings to the screen frame. Be sure the hinges are right side up.

10 Set up your registration guide.

Put the screen in the "up" position. Lay a card on the work surface, and bring the screen down (Figure 13). Adjust the positioning of your card until you're happy with the placement of the image. When you've found the ideal placement, fix the card in place with a piece of drafting tape on the top right side. Tear off two pieces of drafting tape the length of your card, and stick one on top of the other so that one side stays sticky, creating a double-thick piece of tape. Position it so that it runs along the bottom of your card, butting right up against the edge. Repeat this process with two pieces of tape for the left side of your card. This will be your registration guide (Figure 14). The tiny lip created by the double layer of tape will be enough to butt your paper against, allowing your artwork to print in the same spot on every card.

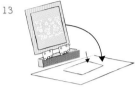

13

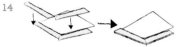

14

11 Print the front of your card with Screen 1.

Mix a container of pale blue ink (Figure 15). Start with several table-spoons of white ink. Add a very small amount of blue ink and stir to mix. Place a card on your work surface, butting it up against your tape guides (Figure 16). With the screen in the "down" position, spoon 1 heaping tablespoon of ink across the top of your screen where the mesh meets the frame, creating an "inkwell" (Figure 17). Lift the screen's bottom edge slightly above the paper; holding your squeegee at a 45-degree angle, push the ink against the top of the screen and then drag the squeegee through the ink and down the screen toward you, applying a thin, even coat. Gently set the screen down, and drag the squeegee down the screen, pressing firmly. Carefully lift your screen and remove the card (Figure 18).

15   16   17   18

To make more prints, quickly drag fresh ink over your screen (lifted slightly off your work surface) to prevent drying, and repeat the above steps, replenishing your ink supply as necessary.

You will need to make a few initial test prints to get a feel for how much ink you'll need and whether you will need to do two passes per print, et cetera. It also takes a few prints for the ink to completely saturate the screen. Make as many prints as necessary, remembering to print about 30 percent more than your desired quantity to allow for errors as the remaining screens are printed.

Set aside your prints as you pull them, and let them dry completely. When finished, wash your screen with a sponge and mild dishwashing soap, and let it dry.

12 Print the backs of your cards with Screen 1 (optional).
Repeat Step 11, printing the floral pattern on the other side of your cards. If desired, print the floral pattern in white ink this time. Rinse Screen 1 out with lukewarm water and a toothbrush, let it dry, apply white ink, and then print.

13 Print the fronts of your cards with Screen 2.
Using a pencil on a test card, mark a line across the bottom of your card, indicating where type should fall, and a vertical line, indicating the center of your card (Figure 19). Repeat Step 10, using these lines to help guide the placement of the artwork on Screen 2 and setting your taped guides accordingly. Repeat Step 11, printing with black ink. Let dry.

19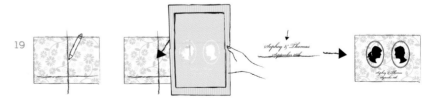

14 Print the backs of your cards with Screen 3.
Repeat Step 12, printing the backs of your cards in black ink using Screen 3.

15 Trim down your cards.

Once your cards are completely dry, trim them down to $4\frac{1}{2}$ x $6\frac{1}{4}$" using a right angle and utility knife. If you are making a large quantity, consider taking them to a copy shop to be cut down with a professional paper cutter.

variations:

Save time on screens. Screen printing is an advanced technique that can take many hours to master. For quicker results, send your artwork to be made into screens for you. It's pretty affordable, and you still reap the rewards of printing your own save the dates, but with half the effort! (See Special Materials by Project, page 140.)

Rubber-stamp return address. Use the typeface from your save the date to have a professional-quality return-address rubber stamp made for your envelopes. This typically costs under $50 and will put the finishing touch on your save the date ensemble (and can be used again and again)! (See Resources, page 139.)

Accommodations cards. Don't forget to let your guests know about travel and hotel arrangements for your wedding. Silk-screen one-sided text-only cards containing travel details, or simply print them on a computer using a matching font and text-weight paper.

Save your screens! Now that you've gone to the effort of learning silk-screening and making your screens, reuse them to decorate other paper goods for your wedding day. Use the silhouette screen to print program covers, cocktail napkins, or the backs of seating cards (boy silhouettes for gentlemen, girl silhouettes for ladies). Use the floral pattern screen to print pretty, patterned coasters and favor tags. Mask with drafting tape any areas you don't want to print.

Name:

Hello!Lucky

(Eunice Moyle and Sabrina Moyle)

Location: San Francisco, California, and London, United Kingdom

See page 45 for Hello!Lucky's complete bio.

AUTHORS Chloe and James Reed

TITLE   Our New Little One

DATE   SEP 0 2 2008

STATS   Mary Jane

         5 lbs. 6 ounces

         21 inches long

9·2·08

Paper + Cup
library book birth announcement
MODERATE

you'll need

Glue stick

Pretty, patterned text-weight paper (trimmed to 6 x 9")

Card stock (trimmed to 6 x 9")

Utility knife

Right angle or ruler

Cutting mat, or a magazine

Bone folder

$8\frac{1}{2}$ x 11" sheet of solid text-weight paper

Scissors

Mailing label (approximately $1\frac{1}{4}$ x $1\frac{3}{4}$")

Rubber-stamp alphabet kit and ink pad or pens

Typewriter or computer with word-processing program and printer

Library card pocket (see Special Materials by Project, page 140)

Photocopier

Library Card template

$8\frac{1}{2}$ x 11" sheet of white or pastel-colored card stock or text-weight paper

Self-inking date stamp

Baby photo (optional)

This "library card" is the perfect birth announcement for book-lovers, teachers, and future teachers' pets. Baby's details fit perfectly, and the card slips into a pocket with a wallet-sized photo. This simple-to-assemble card could be used to invite guests to a baby shower (stamp the expecting mom's "due date" on the library card), or use the card to collect baby name suggestions (make the "title" of the book *Name Ideas for Baby*, and allow guests to fill in names on the blank lines). Regardless of how you adapt this project, it is sure to earn you a gold star!

how to:

1   Cover the card.

Apply glue to the wrong side of the patterned paper. Center the card stock on the patterned paper, doing your best to align the two sheets (there is no need to be perfect, you will be trimming off about $\frac{1}{8}$" on all sides), and smooth to adhere (Figure 1). Using the utility knife, ruler, and cutting mat, trim the papers down to $5\frac{1}{2}$ x 8". Using a bone folder and ruler, score the inside of the card at the halfway mark, and fold it in half (Figure 2).

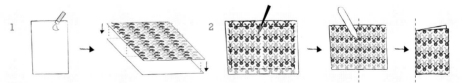

2   Add the spine.

Trim a $\frac{3}{4}$ x $5\frac{3}{4}$" strip of solid-colored text-weight paper. Fold it in half lengthwise. Lay your card flat with the patterned side facing up. Apply glue to the wrong side of the strip, and align the fold in the strip with the fold in your card to create the spine of your "book" (Figure 3). Smooth to adhere, and trim the excess with a ruler and utility knife.

3 Make the corners.
Cut two $^3/_4$" squares from the solid-colored text-weight paper. Cut each square in half diagonally to make four triangles. Apply glue to the back of each triangle, and adhere them to the outside corners of the front and back of your card (Figure 4).

4 Add the title.
Mark the baby's birth date on the mailing label using rubber stamps, pens, or a typewriter. Using the same paper you used for the spine and corners, trim a rectangle $^1/_8$" bigger on all four sides than your mailing label. Center the mailing label on this rectangle, and smooth to adhere. Apply glue to the back of the rectangle, and adhere to the front of your card (Figure 5).

5 Add the library card pocket.
Adhere the library card pocket to the inside back cover of the book (using a glue stick if your pocket doesn't come with a sticky backing) (Figure 6).

6 Make the library card.
Photocopy the Library Card template provided onto card stock (choose white or pastel colors for a classic library look). Using a typewriter, word-processing program, or pen, fill in your library card with the "authors," "title," and stats. If you are using a word-processing program, print out the text, cut out and paste each line within the grid of the blank template, and

photocopy the whole thing. Or, re-create a library card from scratch following the instructions below. Photocopy as many library cards as you will need, and trim them out using a utility knife, ruler, and cutting mat.

7 Stamp the date, and assemble the card.

Using your date stamp, stamp the delivery date onto each library card, preferably in red ink (Figure 7). Tuck the library card into the pocket, and, if desired, insert a 2 x 3" wallet-sized photo (Figure 8).

variations:

Bookish baby shower. With minor adaptations, this card can be turned into an adorable baby shower invitation. Stamp the date of the shower on the cover and, using a typewriter, rubber stamps, or word-processing program, write the event details inside. Title the two columns of the library card *Baby names* and *Due date*, and ask friends to suggest baby names and guess the delivery date. Carry the literary theme throughout the shower by collecting books for baby's library, making bookplates, and creating a keepsake journal for mom. Create a multiple choice "test"—with trivia questions about the new mom—and award gold stars to the winners!

We're expecting! Stamp the words *Special delivery* on the cover, or leave it blank. Use a typewriter, rubber stamps, or word-processing program to write your news on the inside of the card, and use the library card to collect baby name suggestions. If you'd like, include baby pictures of mom and dad in the pocket!

PRINT YOUR OWN LIBRARY CARD

Follow these instructions to make your own library card using Microsoft Word. Print multiples of the cards with a laser or ink-jet printer.

Set up the table.

1   Open a blank document in Microsoft Word.

2   From the main toolbar, select: Table -> Insert -> Table.

3   For Number of Columns, enter 2; for Number of Rows, enter 19.

Name:

Paper + Cup

(Minhee Cho)

Location: Brooklyn, New York

How did you get into crafting and/or card making? I have a graphic design background. I always made my own cards when I was younger, and it just grew into what I do now.

What is your favorite medium? The computer!

What is the most memorable card you've ever received (or sent)? The first card my husband gave me after we became a married couple.

What is your favorite card-sending occasion? Birthdays.

What is the one crafting tool you can't live without? X-Acto knife.

What things most inspire your work? Flea markets.

What Web site is your favorite source of inspiration? www.veer.com.

Where can we find you on the Web? www.papercupdesign.com.

Merge the top four rows.

4 Highlight the top row. From the main menu, select: Table -> Merge Cells.

5 Repeat for the next 3 rows.

Adjust the table size.

6 Hover your cursor over the top of the table until a black downward-pointing arrow appears. Click once on the arrow to highlight the entire table.

7 In the main menu, select Table -> Table Properties. A dialog box will open.

8 In the first screen of the dialog box (Table), check the box marked Preferred Width, and enter 2.7.

9 Click on the Row tab of the dialog box. Check the box marked Specify Height, and enter 0.25. Close the dialog box, and your table's width and height will shrink to the correct size.

Adjust the lines.

10 Hover your mouse over the line that splits the two columns, until you see the double-arrow icon. Click and drag the icon to the left to reduce the width of the left-hand column to about $5/8$".

11 In the main menu, select View -> Toolbars -> Tables and Borders.

12 Select the double-line border from the toolbar's border drop-down menu. A pencil tool will appear. Point the pencil tool to the top edge of the first column in Row 5, and click it to turn the border into a double line. Repeat for the second column in Row 5. Double-click outside the table to go back to your cursor.

Enter the text.

13 Enter the text, using the template provided as a guide. We suggest using an old-school font, such as Courier or Bookman Old Style.

Print and trim the card.

14 Print the card on text-weight paper or card stock. Using a utility knife and ruler, trim the card to size and double-check that it fits in the library pocket, making adjustments to the table size as needed to fit.

The Small Object
humpty dumpty thumbprint card   `BASIC`

you'll need

2 pieces of text-weight paper for the backgrounds (trimmed to 4 x 5¼")

Pencil or pen

Ruler

Ink pad

Photocopier or sheet of 8½ x 11" tracing paper

Humpty Dumpty templates

4 straight pins

3 scraps of fabric, about 1½ x 1½" each (we used 2 pieces of striped fabric for the pants and 1 piece of a different stripe for the hat)

Scissors

Glue stick

1 piece of floral fabric (you'll need 4 different floral motifs to make the flowers growing at the base of Humpty's wall)

4½ x 5¾" folded card

This wonderfully youthful card uses the most basic type of print imaginable—a thumbprint. With the addition of a few scraps of fabric and pencil details, the thumbprint becomes a charming Humpty Dumpty, whose sad fate can aptly convey apologies, sympathy, or regret. But of course, the thumbprint technique can also illustrate cheery occasions!

how to:

1   **Draw the wall.**
    Decide on the placement of your wall. On your first sheet of text-weight background paper (Card 1): Use your pencil or pen and ruler to draw seven parallel, horizontal lines, about 3" long each, spaced evenly ⅛" apart. Decorate the first line with a row of small rectangles (the "bricks")—we drew the rectangles using each row's upper horizontal line as the top edge of that row of bricks, so that each brick is a *U* shape extending down from the line. Continue drawing rows of bricks, spacing them so that each brick falls between two bricks above it (Figure 1). Repeat for all rows.

2   **Place your Humpty.**
    Press your thumb onto the ink pad, and make a thumbprint above your wall—this will be Humpty's body (Figure 2).

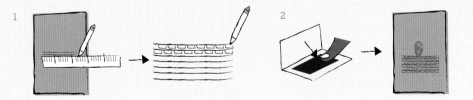

3 Dress your Humpty, and draw his features.

Photocopy or trace the templates for Humpty's pants and hat. Pin the tracing paper or photocopy to your selected fabrics using straight pins, and cut out the hat and pants (Figure 3). Apply glue to the wrong side of the hat and pants, and affix them to your Humpty. With a pencil or pen, add two dots for the eyes, some eyebrows, a nose, a mouth, and two arms (Figure 4).

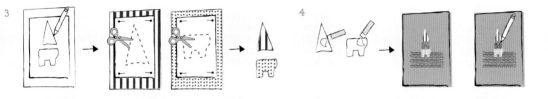

4 Plant some flowers.

Cut four flowers from your flowered fabric (Figure 5). We cut around them very loosely—the imperfection adds to the charmingly naive quality of this card. Apply glue to the wrong side of the fabric, and affix the flowers along the bottom of the wall (Figure 6).

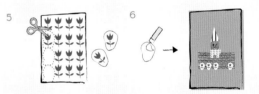

5 Make your Broken Humpty.

Photocopy or trace and cut out the two Broken Humpty stencils (Figure 7). Place Broken Humpty 1 on the left side of your second sheet of background paper (Card 2), with the "broken" edge facing to the right. Press your thumb onto the ink pad, and make a thumbprint over the stencil (half of your thumb should be on the stencil and half on the paper) (Figure 8). Place Broken Humpty 2 on the right side of the paper, making sure the "broken" edge is facing to the left. Press your thumb onto the ink pad, and make a thumbprint over the stencil (half of your thumb on the stencil and half on the paper).

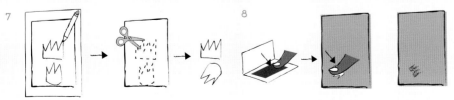

9

6   Dress your Broken Humpty, and draw his features.

Using the stencil you already cut, trace and cut out a second pair of pants for Humpty. Apply glue to the wrong side of the fabric, and adhere to the left side of Broken Humpty. With a pencil or pen, draw the face and arms on the right half of Broken Humpty (Figure 9).

7   Assemble the card, and add a message.

With your glue stick, apply glue to the wrong side of Card 1. Center it on the front of your folded card, and smooth to adhere. Repeat with Card 2, placing it on the inside of the card (Figures 10–12). If you like, add a message on the inside of the card. Or, just leave it blank and let the illustrations convey your sentiment!

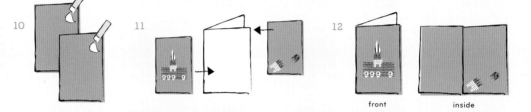

10   11   12

front   inside

variations:

The thumbprint technique is a great starting point for all kinds of amusing cards, especially when you give each thumbprint a distinct personality or character.

Happy holidays from all of us! Orient the card in landscape position and create an entire thumbprint family on the front of the card. Decorate each person with an appropriate pair of pants or skirt, hat, hair, mustache, glasses, et cetera, using fabric scraps and a pencil or pen. Add a Christmas tree, wreath, menorah, or brick fireplace in the background. If your family has a beloved pet, make a thumbprint portrait of him or her inside the card.

First comes love! Draw a tree branch extending from one side of the card, and add two thumbprint characters sitting on the branch, representing you and your honey. Repeat the image on the inside of the card, but place the thumbprint characters so they are touching. Draw faces in profile (with half a mouth and one eye), kissing. If you like, add the greeting, [Name] *and* [Name] *sittin' in a tree . . . K-I-S-S-I-N-G!*

New baby. Create thumbprint portraits of the new parents on the front of the card. Inside, use your pinkie finger for a baby-sized print. Dress the baby in a fabric swaddling cloth.

New home! Draw a simple house on the front of the card, with several large windows. Make thumbprint portraits of family members, peeking out of the windows. Be sure to add the appropriate hats, hair, and features. Add a row of fabric flowers growing in front of the house. On the back of the card (we suggest using a flat card), write your new address and contact details. Be sure to mail the card in an envelope so that the front of the card stays intact.

Name:

The Small Object

(Sarah Neuburger)

Location: Savannah, Georgia

How did you get into crafting and/or card making? Crafting for me was inevitable; growing up, my family made just about everything.

What is your favorite medium? If I could only have one thing, it'd be my pencil and paper.

What is the most memorable card you've ever received (or sent)? A flip-book holiday card I sent with photos of my cat and me, both wearing antlers with bells in a series of photos, taken seconds apart. You can imagine all the squirming and thrashing about my cat was doing.

What is your favorite card-sending occasion? I love the challenge of sending cards around the holidays.

What is the one crafting tool you can't live without? Besides my mechanical pencil, I have a vintage ice pick that is always by my side.

What things most inspire your work? Vintage household items and crafts, textiles, toys, and, perhaps most important, manufacturing processes and materials that I can use on a small scale.

What Web site is your favorite source of inspiration? www.flickr.com.

Where can we find you on the Web? www.thesmallobject.com.

Foxy & Winston
animal print everyday note 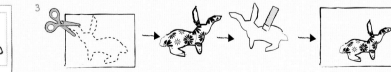 MODERATE

you'll need

Patterned paper or fabric (at least 6 x 8")

Photocopier or toner-based printer

8¹/₂ x 11" sheet of tracing paper

Pencil, 2B or softer

Ballpoint pen

Animal templates

Scissors

Glue stick

Sheet of blank text-weight paper (trimmed to 3¹/₂ x 4⁷/₈")

Gocco machine (see Special Materials by Project, page 140)

2 to 3 Gocco bulbs (see Special Materials by Project, page 140)

2 to 3 Gocco screens (see Special Materials by Project, page 140)

Gocco inks (red and black) (see Special Materials by Project, page 140)

Piece of scrap card stock

6 to 8 pieces of scrap paper for practice runs

3¹/₂ x 4⁷/₈" folded card, folded on the long side

Print Gocco is a basic Japanese screen-printing technique. It is easy to master and allows you to print up to 70 or 80 professional-looking multiples at one time using just a photocopy of the artwork you want to print. While the do-it-yourself machine requires a bit of an investment, you'll be able to reuse it to make large batches of party invitations, holiday cards, personal stationery, and more!

how to:

1 Photocopy your pattern.
Choose a pattern from decorative wrapping paper, wallpaper, or fabric. (We recommend choosing a pattern that is small enough in scale to work inside your animal silhouette.) Make a photocopy of your pattern, or print it on a laser printer (Figure 1). (Gocco screens are made using carbon-based images, so any copier or printer that uses toner will work.)

2 Make your animal, and compose your card.
Trace and transfer (see page 138) your chosen animal template onto the wrong side of your patterned photocopy, making sure your animal will be facing the right way (Figure 2). Cut it out using scissors. Apply glue to the wrong side of your animal, and affix it to your blank text-weight paper, positioning the animal as you'd like it to appear on the card (Figure 3). This is your master.

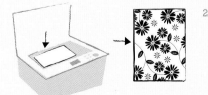

3 Burn your screen.

Align the bottom right corner of your master, faceup, to the top right corner of the pad of your Gocco machine. Follow the manufacturer's instructions for burning your screen. Once you have burned your screen, peel the master off the screen (Figure 4).

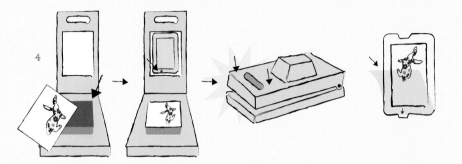

4 Apply ink to your screen.

Remove your Gocco screen from the machine, and lift up the transparent film (Figure 5). Apply a generous quantity of ink over the entire image, being careful not to touch the screen with the tip of the ink tube. Gently spread the ink evenly over the image using a small piece of scrap card stock (Figure 6); the ink will be the consistency of frosting on a cake. Replace the transparent film, and mount the screen into your Gocco machine (Figure 7).

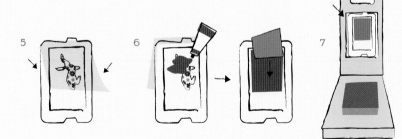

5 Do a few test runs, and print your card.

Place a piece of scrap paper on the pad of your Gocco machine. Lower the screen onto the paper, and press down firmly to print (Figure 8). Lift the screen to view your printed image. It may take a few prints before the entire image will print cleanly. If certain areas don't seem to be printing, add a bit more ink to those areas and try again. Once you are satisfied with the print quality, place your unfolded card on the sticky pad, aligning the bottom right corner of your card with the top right corner of the sticky pad, and print the card. Let it dry.

With enough ink on your screen, you can print 70 or 80 consecutive prints without re-inking. If areas stop printing cleanly, simply reapply ink to those areas and continue printing.

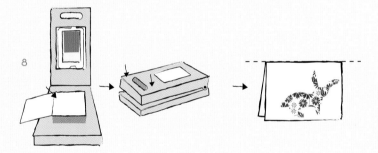

8

variations:

Animal communication. Instead of using a pattern, choose a page of text from a book, or select your own greeting and type it out in repeating rows—creating a pattern of your own with a built-in greeting. Print or photocopy this text, and cut your animal from the resulting pattern.

Children's illustration. In place of the patterned animal, photocopy a picture and/or text drawn by a little friend. Follow the original instructions for printing multiples, perhaps to give as personalized children's stationery.

More Gocco! See A Thoughtful Gesture Thank You Note (page 91) for another project using the Print Gocco technique and for instructions on printing in two colors.

Name:

Foxy & Winston

(Jane Buck)

Location: Brooklyn, New York (hailing originally from England)

How did you get into crafting and/or card making? I worked at Paper Source for a spell, coupled with a background in illustration and textile design.

What is your favorite medium? Definitely screen printing.

What is the most memorable card you've ever received (or sent)? A 1957 postcard that my dad (Winston) etched, depicting a scene on the London Underground. I have it in a frame for all to see.

What is your favorite card-sending occasion? Valentine's Day. I think it brings out the best in the sender.

What is the one crafting tool you can't live without? A bone folder.

What things most inspire your work? The zoo, the Brooklyn Botanic Garden, the Natural History Museum, and David Attenborough's BBC nature documentaries.

What Web site is your favorite source of inspiration? http://designsponge.blogspot.com.

Where can we find you on the Web? www.foxyandwinston.com and www.foxyandwinston.etsy.com.

you'll need

Text-weight paper (to make the example shown, the paper must be 2 x 16"; for larger panels or longer messages, your paper will need to be taller and/or longer)

Ruler

Utility knife

Cutting mat, or a magazine

Pencil

Bone folder

Rubber stamps

Rubber-stamp alphabet kit

Ink pad

Sturdy board (we suggest chipboard or illustration board—enough for two 2¹/₂" squares)

Book cloth or cover-weight paper (enough for two 3¹/₂" squares)

Wax paper

Adhesive (we suggest PVA glue)

Glue brush

Patterned paper (enough for two 2" squares)

3 feet of ribbon

In addition to being a lovely card, the durable board ends of this accordion booklet make it a wonderful keepsake to treasure for years. The message inside literally unfolds, and you can adjust the length of the booklet to tidily fit the length of your note. It's the perfect way to share a sentiment, thought, or secret!

how to:

PART ONE: MAKE THE PANELS

1 Choose the number of panels.

The number of panels will depend on what you want to say. Once you've established your message, you'll need to figure out how many panels (pages) you will need to express it. Keep in mind that you'll need an even number of panels in order for the book to close properly. Also, you'll need an extra panel at each end to use as bookends, both of which will be covered in decorative paper. The example shown on page 84 uses eight panels (four panels to express the message, plus two bookend panels).

2 Measure and cut a paper strip to form the accordion panels.

The height of your panel strip should equal the height of your cover, minus ¹/₂". The length of your panel strip should equal the width of your cover, minus ¹/₂" and multiplied by the number of panels. Don't forget to include two extra panels for bookends. In the example shown, the panel strip measures 2" high x 16" long, forming six 2"-square panels, plus the bookends (Figures 1–2).

3 Fold the paper strip into panels.

Use your ruler and pencil to make a light mark on the long side of your paper strip, indicating the width of a single panel. Fold your strip of paper from left to right at this mark. Continue folding back and forth until you have accordion-folded your entire strip, using your bone folder to make strong creases (Figure 2).

4 Write a message on the panels.

Using your stamps and ink, create a special message on the panels, remembering that the farthest left and farthest right panels will not be part of the finished design (Figure 3). Set your panel strip aside.

3

PART TWO: MAKE THE COVERS AND ENDPAPERS

5 Cut out the book-cover boards.

Using your ruler and utility knife, cut two pieces of sturdy board to the exact same size to make the covers. The example shown measures $2\frac{1}{2}$ x $2\frac{1}{2}$". Set the pieces aside.

6 Cut out book cloth to wrap the book-cover boards.

Using your utility knife or scissors, cut two cover sheets from book cloth, each sheet $\frac{1}{2}$" larger on all four sides than your cover boards. Center one cover board on the back of a cover sheet. Using a pencil, lightly trace the outline of the board onto the book cloth (Figure 4). Trim the corners to 45-degree angles, leaving two times the cover board's thickness between the board and the cut line (Figure 5). This will leave you with four book-cloth flaps.

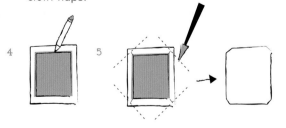

4   5

7 Cover the front cover with book cloth.

Lay down a sheet of wax paper on your work surface. Place your book cloth on the wax paper with the wrong side facing up. Brush a thin, even coat of adhesive inside the pencil outline on your book cloth. Make sure to spread the glue all the way to the edges. Lay the book-cover board onto the glued cover cloth, centered inside the pencil outline. Press firmly. Turn the piece over. Using your bone folder, rub the cloth from the center, working outward, smoothing out any air bubbles. Add a bit more glue to the book-cloth flaps on the long sides. (If all sides are the same length, start with the top and bottom.) Working quickly before the glue dries, glue down the flaps, folding them over the edge of the board. Repeat with the short sides (Figure 6). Using the tip of your bone folder, tuck in the excess book cloth at the corners.

6
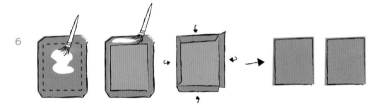

8 Wrap the back cover.

Repeat Step 7 for the back cover.

9 Cut out decorative endpapers.

Cut two pieces from your patterned paper, $1/8$" smaller than your cover on all four sides. These endpapers will cover the accordion panels that are glued to the front and back covers. Set aside.

PART THREE: ASSEMBLE THE BOOK

10 Adhere the accordion panels to the book covers.

Brush a thin, even coat of adhesive on the back side of the first panel of your message (Figure 7). Center this panel onto the back of the front cover board. Using your bone folder, rub from the center, working outward, smoothing out any air bubbles. Repeat for the back panel (Figure 8).

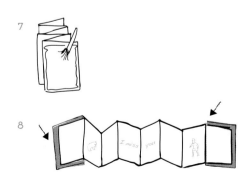

11 Adhere the endpapers to the book covers.

Brush a thin, even coat of glue on the wrong side of your endpapers. Center one endpaper on the inside of each cover—they should completely cover the panels you just glued down (Figure 9). Press the endpapers firmly onto the cover board, and smooth out any air bubbles with the bone folder.

12 Let the booklet dry.

Slide a small piece of wax paper between the front and back panels to keep any excess glue from sticking to the other panels. Set the book aside to dry for at least 30 minutes. We suggest putting a heavy book on top of the accordion book to flatten it as it dries.

13 Make a ribbon closure.

Fold your ribbon in half. On the back cover of your book, dab a straight line of adhesive across the middle. Place the ribbon on the glue, leaving equal lengths on either side of the cover (Figure 10); press the ribbon firmly into place with the bone folder. Let it dry.

14 Finish the card.

Once the booklet and ribbon are dry, wrap the loose ends of the ribbon around the front of the book and tie it into a bow (Figure 11). To mail the card, place it in a small mailing box (see Resources, page 139) or padded envelope; line the box with tissue paper or excess patterned paper from your endpapers.

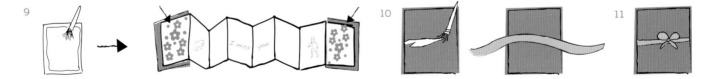

variations:

A thoughtful occasion. This project can be used for almost any occasion, but we think it's especially great for those occasions that call for a truly thoughtful and personal sentiment (it's quite a bit of work, after all).

Size it up (or down!). This card can be made to any size, including one that fits snugly in a square envelope for mailing. To fit it into a standard 5$\frac{3}{4}$" square envelope, make the cover boards 5$\frac{1}{4}$ x 5$\frac{1}{4}$" (leaving plenty of room to accommodate the thickness of the card).

Wedding invitation. For those readers who are truly ambitious (and engaged to be married), we've seen this format used to create stunning wedding invitations—just make sure you size it to fit an available envelope size and have a bevy of crafty bridesmaids on hand to help out (or plan a very small wedding!).

Name:

Pancake & Franks

(Stacy Pancake and Nicole Passerotti)

Location: San Francisco, California

How did you get into crafting and/or card making? In response to the dying art of paper correspondence.

What is your favorite medium? Paper.

What is the most memorable card you've ever received (or sent)? **Stacy Pancake:** A handwritten card from my little brother, with stickers, stamps, and misspelled words and bursting with excitement.

What is your favorite card-sending occasion? My favorite special occasion to send a card is having no occasion at all.

What is the one crafting tool you can't live without? A bone folder.

What things most inspire your work? Nature, friends, and good stories.

What Web site is your favorite source of inspiration? http://hopingforhappyaccidents.blogspot.com.

Where can we find you on the Web? www.pancakeandfranks.com.

you'll need

Photocopier

Hand-and-Frame templates

Ruler

Utility knife or scissors

Cutting mat, or a magazine

Print Gocco machine (see Special Materials by Project, page 140)

5 to 6 Gocco bulbs (see Special Materials by Project, page 140)

3 to 4 Gocco screens (see Special Materials by Project, page 140)

2 Gocco ink colors (we used red and black) (see Special Materials by Project, page 140)

Piece of scrap card stock

6 to 8 pieces of scrap paper for practice runs

3$\frac{1}{2}$ x 4$\frac{7}{8}$" folded card, folded on the long side

Felt-tip pen

With its elegant hand and dainty frame, this card is a lovely way to convey your personal thoughts. Choose from the variety of hand-and-frame stencils provided, and use Print Gocco, a basic Japanese screen-printing technique, to print as many cards as you need. Then, write a greeting for your special occasion (by hand, of course!).

how to:

1 Make your art.
Photocopy the Hand-and-Frame templates provided for both color layers of your card. With a ruler and utility knife, trim your paper to the registration frame around the templates, making sure to cut off the registration lines so that they don't transfer to your screen (Figure 1). These will be your masters.

2 Burn Screen 1.
Align the bottom right corner of your first master faceup to the top right corner of the pad of your Gocco machine. Follow the manufacturer's instructions for burning your screen. Once you have burned your screen, peel the master off the screen (Figure 2).

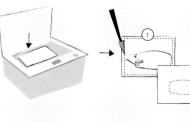

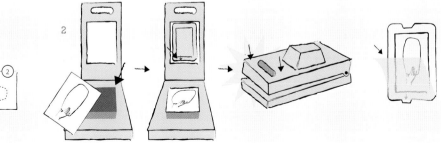

3 Apply ink to your screen.

Remove your Gocco screen from the machine, and lift up the transparent film (Figure 3). Apply a generous quantity of ink over your entire image, being careful not to touch the screen with the tip of the ink tube. Gently spread the ink evenly over the image with a small piece of scrap card stock (Figure 4); the ink will be the consistency of frosting on a cake. Replace the transparent film, and mount the screen into your Gocco machine (Figure 5).

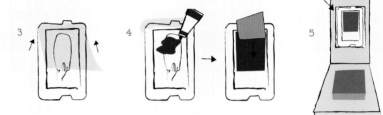

4 Do a few test runs, and print the first color of your card.

Place a piece of scrap paper on the pad of your Gocco machine. Lower the screen onto your paper, and press down firmly to print (Figure 6). Lift the screen to view your printed image. It may take a few prints before the entire image will print cleanly. If certain areas don't seem to be printing, add a bit more ink to those areas and try again. Once you are satisfied with the print quality, place your unfolded card on the sticky pad, aligning the bottom right corner of your card with the top right corner of the sticky pad and ensuring that the top of the image is about $1/8$" from the fold in the card. Print your card, and let it dry.

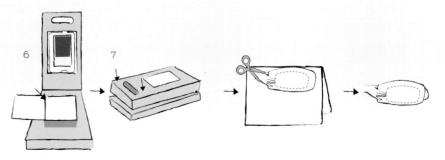

With enough ink on your screen, you can print 70 or 80 consecutive prints without re-inking. If areas stop printing cleanly, simply reapply ink to those areas and continue printing.

5 Burn Screen 2 and print the second color.
Repeat Steps 2–4 with the artwork for the second color.

6 Handwrite your greeting, and cut out the card.
Write your greeting using a felt-tip pen. Fold the finished card, and carefully trim around the artwork using a utility knife or scissors, leaving a $1/8$" border around the artwork and the fold at the top of the card intact (Figure 7).

variations:

A thoughtful gift. This card makes a lovely gift enclosure. Using a photo-copier, scale down the Hand-and-Frame templates to fit a small enclosure-sized card (approximately 2 x $3^1/_2$"). Write the recipient's name in the frame, or the words *For you*. After you have completed your card, punch a hole in the top left corner, thread a pretty ribbon through the hole, and attach the card to your gift.

Creative clip art. Clip-art books are a great source for creative images, including fancy frames, flowers, birds, and hands in different gestures (see Resources, page 139). Photocopy and cut out the clip-art images that you like. If needed, glue separate images down on a fresh sheet of copy paper, and make a new copy of the composite image. If you are printing layers in different colors, make a separate photocopy for each layer. Then hold the photocopies up to the light until they are aligned. Tape the pieces together, mark out the outline of the front of your card, and trim to size.

Name:

Julianna Swaney

Location: Manchester, Michigan

How did you get into crafting and/or card making? I've been making cards since I could hold a pair of scissors, but I really got into it when I discovered the wonders of the Gocco printer in college.

What is your favorite medium? Pencil on paper.

What is the most memorable card you've ever received (or sent)? I got a musical card for my birthday once; I saved it for years in a drawer. Every now and then, it would scare me to death by just bursting into song all by itself.

What is your favorite card-sending occasion? I'm bad at remembering to send cards on occasions. I prefer sending everyday cards to say *Hello*.

What is the one crafting tool you can't live without? A blender marker: the special pen I use to transfer photocopies onto drawing paper.

What things most inspire your work? Anything and everything Victorian.

What Web site is your favorite source of inspiration? www.etsy.com.

Where can we find you on the Web? www.ohmycavalier.com.

Abigail Brown

new baby nest card MODERATE

you'll need

4¹/₂ x 6¹/₄" folded card

Ruler

Utility knife

Cutting mat, or a magazine

5 x 7" piece of card stock

Pencil

8¹/₂ x 11" sheet of tracing paper

Nest Card stencils

6 scraps of colored or patterned text-weight paper, approximately 4 x 4"

3 to 4 scraps of fabric, approximately 3 x 3"

Scissors

Rubber-stamp alphabet kit

Ink pad

Glue stick

Needle

Three to four 12" pieces of thread in various colors

With just a few basic shapes to cut, this pretty, collaged card is easy to multiply if you want to send a birth announcement to many recipients. The vintage-inspired papers and fabrics feel warm and familiar—the perfect materials to adorn such a happy message. Hand-stitching lends an inviting, homemade touch, and a puffy cumulus cloud carries the dreamy news of baby's arrival! Handwrite your message, or keep it assembly-line simple by using rubber stamps.

how to:

1 Cut out the front of the card.

Start with a blank folded card; this is Card 1. Use your ruler, utility knife, and cutting mat to cut out a second piece of card stock the exact same size as Card 1 folded in half. This is Card 2, on which you will adhere your design (Figure 1).

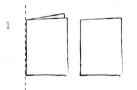

2 Trace the birds, nest, cloud, and leaves.

Using a pencil and tracing paper, trace the Nest, Cloud, Mama Bird (including the Wing and Tail Feather), Baby Bird, and Leaf stencils pro-vided. Lay the tracing paper shapes over your collage papers and fabrics. In the example on page 94, we used fabric for leaves and one of the tail feathers, and paper for the other shapes. Trace the shapes more than once if you would like more than one to work with.

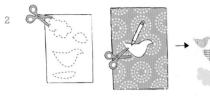
2

3 Cut out the shapes.

Cut out the pieces using scissors or a utility knife and cutting mat (Figure 2). Don't worry too much about following the lines exactly; imperfections add character!

4 Stamp your message on the cloud, and attach the shapes to the card.

Using your rubber-stamp alphabet kit and ink pad, stamp your message on the cloud (Figure 3). Arrange the shapes on Card 2. Once you're happy with the arrangement, apply glue to the back of each piece, and press down firmly (Figure 4).

5 Stitch the legs, nest, leaves, and feathers.

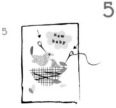
5

Add details to the nest, leaves, and birds by stitching through the card using a needle and thread (see Simple Sewing, page 137) (Figure 5). In this example, we added a few stitches to the mama bird's chest, wings, and tail and gave her two stitched legs. We also added stitches to the nest and the center of each leaf.

6 Make the birds' eyes and add other details.

Add extra details by pricking your needle through Card 2 to make small holes for the birds' eyes (Figure 5). Add pricked holes in other places as you see fit to lend more texture to the card.

7 Glue the cards together.

Glue Card 2 to the front of Card 1, aligning the edges (Figure 6). If necessary, use your ruler, utility knife, and cutting mat to trim the edges of the card so that the two cards align. Lay the card flat, and allow it to dry for at least 30 minutes. We suggest putting a heavy book on top to flatten it as the glue dries.

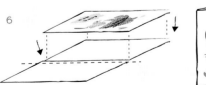
6

variations:

New baby girl, boy, twins (or more!). Alter the color palette to signify a girl or a boy, and change the message accordingly. For multiple babies, add an extra baby bird to the nest.

New nest! To congratulate a friend on a new home, follow all the instructions but leave out the baby bird. If the friends are a couple, cut out a second adult bird and place the two birds in the nest together (see Lovebirds below).

Lovebirds. Leave out the baby bird and add a second adult bird, touching beaks with the first bird. Cut out a small heart shape, and glue it above the two birds.

Design your own. Using the same materials and techniques, cut out freehand shapes to make your own design. An ice cream cone, layer cake, and doughnut (with stitched sprinkles!) are all easy to make and lend themselves perfectly to this technique—as well as to a variety of occasions.

Name:
Abigail Brown

Location: London, United Kingdom

How did you get into crafting and/or card making? I grew up spending days on end with my grandma, who was a hard-working seamstress. From an early age, I found a lot of fun in snipping, sticking, sewing, and general mess-making.

What is your favorite medium? Fabric and stitch.

What is the most memorable card you've ever received (or sent)? An artist friend gave me the most beautiful card, a really lovely design of hers that she had printed. But what was truly memorable was the message, assuring me that our some-times-criticized artistic path was the right one. It was one of the most beautiful and inspiring things I have ever received.

What is your favorite card-sending occasion? Random occasions—I like getting surprises in the post!

What is the one crafting tool you can't live without? Sewing machine.

What things most inspire your work? Many of the fabulous children's book illustrators working today. Mostly art that is pictorial, and in some cases naive and childlike, like someone's mind spilled over onto paper.

What Web site is your favorite source of inspiration? http://printpattern.blogspot.com.

Where can we find you on the Web? www.abigailbrown.etsy.com, www.myspace.com/abigailbrownscreatures, and www.abigail-brown.co.uk.

François Vigneault

wish you were here! postcard set

BASIC

you'll need

Two to three 8 1/2 x 11" sheets of card stock

Utility knife

Ruler

Cutting mat, or a magazine

Map of your trip

Pencil

Scissors

Glue stick or double-sided tape

Marker

1 x 3" (or similar) multipurpose labels, or 1 sheet of text-weight paper to make your own labels

1 to 2 pieces of scrap paper (trimmed to small triangles)

Typewriter (optional)

Various rubber stamps (optional)

Ink pads (optional)

Pens

Postage

The good old-fashioned road trip: wind in your hair, scenery rushing by, the thrill of exploration! Keep your loved ones clued in on your adventures by sending these fabulous multipart map postcards along the way. Assemble the postcards before you take off, and then pop them in mailboxes along the way. Bon voyage!

how to:

1 **Trim the card stock to postcard size.**
   Your final card size can be anywhere between 3 1/2 x 5" and 4 1/4 x 6" and still be sent at the U.S. postcard rate. (You can always go bigger if you don't mind paying the letter rate!) Many craft stores sell precut card stock in postcard size. If yours isn't precut, use a utility knife and ruler to cut five postcards to size (Figure 1). (See Postcard Design Tips, page 100, for tips on making sure your postcard meets U.S. Postal Service requirements.)

2 **Map your route.**
   Using your cut card-stock pieces as size templates, figure out which sections of the map you want to showcase. The pieces should be more or less contiguous so that the recipients can trace your route as they receive the cards. Tracing your card-stock pieces, lightly outline your chosen map sections in pencil (you can erase any marks later) (Figure 2).

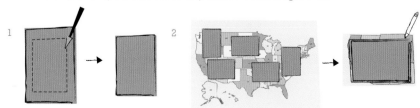

- Make your postcard no smaller than $3^1/_2$ x 5" and no larger than $4^1/_4$ x 6" in order to mail it at the postcard rate.

- Make sure the card's aspect ratio (length divided by width) is between 1.3 and 2.4, otherwise it may need additional postage.

- If you use a dividing line to separate the address from the text on the back of the card, make sure it is at least 4" from the right side of the card. The address area should also be clear of extraneous text (graphics are okay).

- In the bottom right corner of the back of the card, leave a $^5/_8$ x 5" blank space for the post office bar code.

5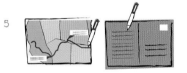

3   Cut out and attach the map pieces.

Using your scissors, cut out the map sections, leaving a $^1/_{16}$" border around each piece (Figure 3); this excess will come in handy as you continue. Using a strong glue stick or double-sided tape, adhere the cut map sections to the card stock. The easiest way to get flush edges is to lay your map section on your work surface, wrong side facing up. Apply a thin, even coat of glue on your card, making sure to spread the glue all the way to the edges. Center the card on the map section and press firmly to adhere. Trim off any excess map (Figure 4).

3 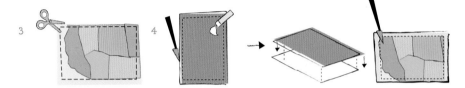 4

4   Decorate the maps.

In the example shown on page 98, we went over the proposed route with a red marker as we completed each leg of the trip (Figure 5). The labels were placed in advance at various points of interest; the pointers are just little triangles of paper glued onto the map. We decorated the labels with type-written captions and some fun rubber stamps, but you could even add little drawings or items you've collected on the road (matchbook covers, photo-booth snapshots, et cetera); just bring along some double-sided tape.

5   Decorate the postcard backs.

Give the back of the postcard a classic look with a dividing line and a designated space for the address (Figure 5). We added the *POSTCARD* label using a rubber-stamp alphabet kit and the address lines using a pen. We also added a *1 of 5* notation to let the recipient know that more missives were on the way. Don't forget to add the postage before you leave for your trip!

variations:

Not planning a trip anytime soon? Never fear! This idea can be adapted in all kinds of ingenious ways. The key is to let the recipient collect the cards over time, piecing them together like a puzzle.

Art installment. Cut out sections of a favorite poster or print, highlighting areas that are intriguing on their own and that also fit together to make a complete picture.

Surprise! Use the card as a teaser for a birthday or anniversary gift (or even a marriage proposal!). Select images (from magazines, newspapers, maps, or other printed materials) for each card that serve as hints about what's to come. Write a clue or note on the other side.

Treasure map. Create a treasure map that leads to a fabulous discovery (say, to a venue for a sold-out event, a surprise party, or your garage for an exciting weekend road trip). Have each map lead to the place where the next card is hidden. The final card leads to the big treasure!

Collected genius. Send a series or collection. Create your postcards from a collection of pulp-fiction book covers, drawings from vintage sewing-pattern envelopes, or a truly fantastic magazine spread. The entire collection can be displayed as a cluster of tiny works of art!

Name:

François Vigneault

Location: San Francisco, California

How did you get into crafting and/or card making? I have always loved drawing and making illustrated cards and letters, but I really got into paper crafting in the last few years, when I started self-publishing comics and 'zines.

What is your favorite medium? Comics.

What is the most memorable card you've ever received (or sent)? I once found an adorable vintage greeting card with a sad little girl saying, *Be Careful . . . It's My Heart.* I saved it for two years before finding the right person to give it to (my wonderful girlfriend, Hannah).

What is your favorite card-sending occasion? I love to send cards and letters to people out of the blue, just when you happen to think of them.

What is the one crafting tool you can't live without? Double-sided tape.

What things most inspire your work? Friendship, nature, and books.

What is your favorite source of inspiration? I'm so inspired after I go to a comics, 'zine, or craft festival. The grassroots creativity on display is tremendous, and there is always something that I've never seen before.

Where can we find you on the Web? www.family-style.com.

happy holidays from the smith family

Amy Karol

photo ornament holiday card

BASIC

you'll need

1 sheet of double-sided scrapbooking paper (trimmed to $6^{1}/_{4}$ x 9") or 1 patterned sheet and 1 solid sheet

Ruler or right angle

Bone folder

Scissors

Scallop-edged scissors

Sheet of colored text-weight paper (trimmed to $3^{1}/_{8}$ x $6^{1}/_{4}$")

Pencil

Eraser

$^{1}/_{8}$" hole punch

Pens or rubber-stamp alphabet kit and ink pad

Glue stick

Sheet of text-weight kraft (natural brown) paper (trimmed to $3^{3}/_{8}$ x $6^{1}/_{4}$")

Circle cutter

Photograph (make sure the area you want to feature will fit in a $1^{3}/_{4}$" circle)

2" round wood tag (see Special Materials by Project, page 140)

12" length of baker's twine or thin ribbon (see Special Materials by Project, page 140)

This charming holiday card is easy to multiply, and the wood tag doubles as an adorable photo ornament! To save time when making multiples, choose a double-sided scrapbooking paper for the main card, and photocopy or print (using a computer and printer) your greeting onto sheets of colored text-weight paper. Then, trim the sheets to the dimensions required for the project.

how to:

1 Make Card 1.

If you are using double-sided scrapbooking paper, score it at the halfway mark, parallel to the long side, using a ruler and bone folder, so that your paper folds down to a $4^{1}/_{2}$ x $6^{1}/_{4}$" landscape-format card (Figure 1). If you are using two sheets of paper, double-paste your papers together (see Double-Pasting, page 134), trim to $6^{1}/_{4}$ x 9", and score and fold as per the instructions above. With your scallop-edged scissors, trim about $^{1}/_{4}$" off only the front edge of your card. When closed, the scalloped edge of the card will reveal the contrasting paper inside (Figure 1).

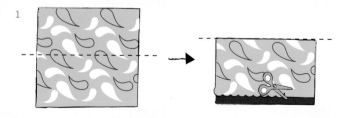

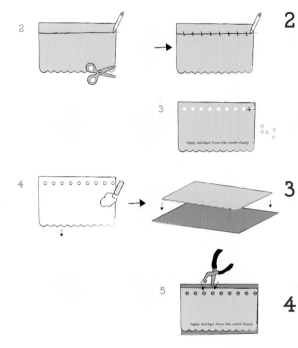

2 Make Card 3.

With your scallop-edged scissors, trim about $1/8$" off one long edge of the colored text-weight paper. With a ruler or right angle and a pencil, draw a straight line on the front of the card, parallel to the top, about $3/8$" from the edge. Measure and mark the line, starting about $3/8$" from the edge of your paper. Space the marks evenly, $1/4$" apart (Figure 2). Using your hole punch, punch a hole at each mark. The result should be a row of evenly spaced holes. Write or rubber-stamp your greeting along the scalloped edge (Figure 3).

3 Attach Card 3 to Card 2.

Apply glue to the wrong side of Card 3 and affix it to the kraft paper (Card 2), leaving a $1/8$" border at the top and bottom (Figure 4). Align your hole punch with the third hole from the left (Hole 3), and punch through Card 2. Repeat with the fourth hole from the left (Hole 4) (Figure 5). You will string your ornament through these holes.

4 Assemble the ornament.

Align your circle cutter to the appropriate area on your photo, and cut a $1 3/4$" circle (Figure 6). Align the circular photo and wood tag and, using a pencil on the back of the photograph, mark where the hole should go. Punch a hole through the photo (Figure 7). Apply glue to the back of the photo and center it on your wood tag, aligning the holes. Smooth to adhere. Let it dry for about 30 minutes. Thread the baker's twine through the tag, and tie right over left (as if you are making the first tie of a knot) (Figure 8). Thread the left end of the string through Hole 3 and the right end through Hole 4, working front to back (Figure 9). Pull until your tag is in approximately the right position, with the bottom of the tag falling about $3/4$" from the bottom edge of the card. Thread the right end through Hole 3 and the left through Hole 4, and adjust so that both sides are even in length. Tie a bow (Figure 10).

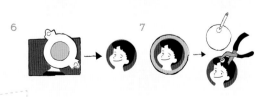

5 Assemble your card.

Apply glue to the wrong side of Card 2, and affix it to the front of Card 1, positioning Card 2 about $^3/_8$" down from the folded top edge of Card 1 and flush on either side (Figure 11).

11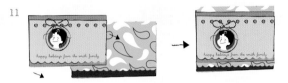

variations:

This card can be varied myriad ways simply by layering different types of papers and using different types of decorative-edged scissors or tags. In fact, if you're making multiples, you may want to consider doing a few variations to keep things fresh.

Keepsake birth announcement. With a photo of the newborn or a rubber-stamped initial, the ornament becomes a charming keepsake. To make it feel even more precious, scale down the card and, to save time, make it flat rather than folded. Look for a $1^1/_2$" wood tag. Trim Card 1 to $3^1/_2$ x 5", or leave $1/_2$" excess on all sides, mark out the finished size, and trim with scallop-edged scissors. Print or photocopy the baby's birth details on the right half of Card 2, then trim to 3 x $4^1/_2$". Punch holes and affix the ornament. Glue Card 2 to Card 1, revealing a $1/_4$" border on all sides.

Nostalgic birthday. Use this card to celebrate a milestone birthday. Affix a photo of the birthday girl or boy to the tag, preferably a humorous candid shot from back in the day. Rubber-stamp the date on the back of the tag, and write a funny quip about how they haven't changed one bit!

Name:

Amy Karol

Location: Portland, Oregon

How did you get into crafting and/or card making? I have been crafting ever since I can remember. I started card making pretty seriously in college when I was getting into bookbinding. I love sewing, so bookbinding was a natural step for me. Then box making and papermaking . . . and now, with three kids, cards are more my speed.

What is your favorite medium? Sewing (like in my book, *Bend-the-Rules Sewing*) and working with fabric, but I love paper, painting, everything.

What is the most memorable card you've ever received (or sent)? A rubber fish with a tag around the neck. One side of the tag had a postage stamp, the other side had my address. That was it. It made my day, and my postal carrier thought it was the coolest thing ever.

What is your favorite card-sending occasion? Christmas!

What is the one crafting tool you can't live without? My Fiskars paper trimmer. I have two and would marry them if I could.

What things most inspire your work? History. I love old ephemera, magazines, books, labels, and packaging.

What Web site is your favorite source of inspiration? Too many to count! I love all the paper crafting sites, especially ones about paper toys. And I troll eBay for folk/outsider art.

Where can we find you on the Web? www.amykarol.com, www.angrychicken.typepad.com, and www.kingpod.com.

big number birthday card [BASIC]

you'll need

4 1/2 x 6 1/4" folded card

Decorative rubber stamp

Ink pad

3 to 4 pieces of scrap paper (approximately 6 x 8")

Drafting tape

4" number stencil (see Special Materials by Project, page 140), or make your own (see below)

Acrylic or tempera paint

Paper plate

Stencil brush, small foam paint roller, or paintbrush

Fine paintbrush (optional)

Fine-point permanent marker

Photograph (optional)

Pencil

Utility knife (optional)

Cutting mat, or a magazine (optional)

To make your own stencil (optional):

Computer printer

Drafting tape

2 to 3 sheets of acetate or Mylar, approximately 4 1/2 x 6 1/4" (see Special Materials by Project, page 140)

Utility knife

These bold number cards are great for big birthdays, invitations, and announcements. What's more, you can make them using inexpensive materials from your local hardware store. House-number stencils, acrylic house paint (available in sample sizes), and paint rollers are all just right for the job!

how to:

1   Make your background.

Lay the card flat on your work surface, right side up. With your decorative rubber stamp, stamp across the card to create a background pattern (Figure 1).

2   Make your own number stencil (optional).

Using a computer and printer, print out a number in a solid typeface that you like, sized to fit nicely on the front of your card (about 350–400 point size). Lay the printout on your cutting surface, and tape it down. Next, tape a sheet of acetate or Mylar over it (Figure 2). With your utility knife, carefully cut through the acetate, tracing the outer edge of your number (Figure 3). If your number has negative space (such as the inside of a *0*), leave a small strip of acetate adjoining the negative space to the rest of the stencil. When you have cut around the entire number, lift up the acetate sheet and push out the cutout portions. The acetate with the number punched out will be your stencil.

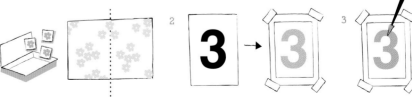

Note: Try Steps 3 and 4 on scrap paper before working with your rubber-stamped card.

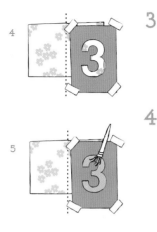

3 Position your stencil.

Lay the card, right side up and flat, on your work surface and tape the corners down. Lay your stencil on top of the card, positioning the number as you'd like it to appear on the front of the card. Tape the edges of your stencil down securely (Figure 4).

4 Print your number.

Squeeze a quarter-sized dollop of paint onto a paper plate and apply a thin, even coat to your stencil brush or roller. Make sure you don't pick up too much paint so it doesn't bleed under the stencil. Holding the stencil in place with one hand, brush an even coat of paint over your stencil (Figure 5). Set aside the brush, and carefully lift off the stencil.

If the edges are fuzzy, you can clean or sharpen them using a fine paintbrush. If the paint is seeping under the stencil, reduce the amount of paint on your roller and try again. Let your card dry thoroughly. If you are printing multiple cards, make sure your stencil is dry on both sides before making another print.

5 Decorate the card.

Using a fine-point permanent marker, outline the number and rubber-stamped pattern. Draw freehand vertical lines, spaced about $1/8$" apart, to create a textured background (Figure 6).

6 Cut slits for a photograph (optional).

Place the photo inside the card, and mark the top right and lower left corners of the photo with a pencil. Cut a slit diagonal to the two corners using a utility knife (Figure 7). Make the slits just wide enough that the photo corners will tuck in and hold the photo securely.

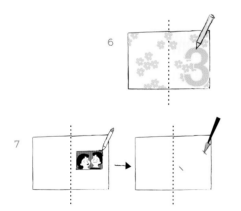

variations:

You're invited! These cards can double as birthday or anniversary party invitations. In place of a photo, insert a piece of paper with a handwritten or computer-generated message.

Desktop frame. Turn the card into a desktop frame by taking the photo out of the inner slits and inserting it into the slits on the patterned side (back) of the card. Bend the card slightly against the original crease so that it will sit upright on a table or desk.

ABCs. In place of a number stencil, select a letter stencil. For a birthday card or birth announcement, paint the recipient's or new baby's first initial. For a valentine, paint the letter *L* on the outside of the card and rubber-stamp *is for love* on the inside.

Name:

Binth

Location: Chicago, Illinois

How did you get into crafting and/or card making? We were a design and art service company looking to produce a commercial product that combined our love of skilled craftsmanship with design.

What is your favorite medium? Screen printing.

What is the most memorable card you've ever received (or sent)? An elaborate foldout card that revealed hidden maps and sights for a town in Germany.

What is your favorite card-sending occasion? Christmas.

What is the one crafting tool you can't live without? A computer.

What things most inspire your work? It ranges from everyday objects to modern design and art.

What Web site is your favorite source of inspiration? Everything from design blogs to eBay!

Where can we find you on the Web? www.binth.com.

blue-ribbon badge congratulations card — BASIC

you'll need

1 yard of 1¹/₂" or 2" ribbon

Sewing needle

18" of thread

Scissors

6" of contrasting 1" ribbon

Button (³/₄" or larger)

Piece of card stock (large enough from which to cut a 1¹/₂" circle)

Craft glue

1" bar pin with safety catch (see Special Materials by Project, page 140)

Glue stick

Pretty, patterned paper (trimmed to 6¹/₂ x 9¹/₄")

Card stock (trimmed to 6¹/₂ x 9¹/₄")

Utility knife

Ruler

Cutting mat, or a magazine

Bone folder

Rubber-stamp alphabet kit and ink pad or pens

Pay tribute to a pal's crowning achievement with this colorful card that doubles as a festive, wearable badge. Choose fabrics and patterns that fit the occasion—necktie stripes for Father's Day, dark blues for graduation—as well as the wearer!

how to:

1 Make your rosette.

Fold one end of your ribbon four to five times back and forth accordion-style, with each fold about ¹/₄" wide (Figure 1). Holding the ribbon in place with your fingers, pierce it ¹/₄" from one edge with a needle and thread (see Simple Sewing, page 137). Pull the thread all the way through (Figure 2). Take the next portion of the ribbon and make four to five more folds. Pierce ¹/₄" from the edge of the next folds with your needle, and pull the thread through. Repeat, making four to five folds at a time. The fabric should fan out on the open (unstitched) side until you have a nice rosette (Figure 3). When you are happy with the way your rosette looks, trim the end of the ribbon with the scissors. Match up the open edges, and sew the rosette along the joined edge (Figure 4).

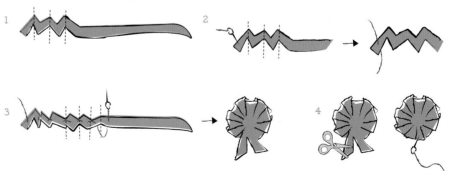

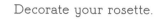

2 **Decorate your rosette.**
Fold your contrasting ribbon in half, and adjust the fold so that it has two distinct tails (it should look like an upside down *V*) (Figure 5). Sew this to the back of your rosette, and trim both tails to a 45-degree angle. Position your button in the center of the rosette, and sew it in place (see Simple Sewing, page 137) (Figure 6).

3 **Assemble the badge.**
Cut a 1 1/2" circle from your small piece of card stock. Apply some craft glue to this circle and center it on the back of your rosette. Press to adhere. Apply a small amount of craft glue to your bar pin and center it on the circle, pressing to adhere (Figure 7). Let it dry for 30 minutes.

4 Make the card.
Using a glue stick, apply glue to the wrong side of the patterned paper. Center the card stock on the patterned paper, doing your best to align the two sheets (it needn't be perfect, you'll be trimming off about 1/8" on all sides), and smooth to adhere (Figure 8). Using the utility knife, ruler, and cutting mat, trim the card down to 6 1/4 x 9". Using a bone folder and ruler, score the inside of the card at the halfway mark, and fold it in half.

5 Assemble the card, and write your message.
Decide where you'll want your badge to sit on the front of the card. Place two marks in the approximate spots where the bar pin will pierce the card. Using the utility knife, cut two small slits at these marks. Pin your badge to the card, piercing through the two slits (Figure 9). With your rubber-stamp alphabet kit, stamp your message on the inside of the card, or write the message by hand. We like *You're the best* or *You're #1!*

variations:

#1 Dad or #1 Mom. For Dad, choose traditional masculine patterns for the card and badge: necktie stripes, houndstooth, argyle, plaid. For Mom, choose feminine florals or pretty patterns. Rubber-stamp or write *#1 Mom* or *#1 Dad* on the inside of the card.

Extra-fancy badge. For an extra-special pal or occasion, make a double rosette, using two contrasting types of ribbon. Lay the smaller ribbon on top of the larger one, flush to one edge. Make four to five folds with the double ribbon, and pierce 1/4" up from the flush edge, using your needle and thread. Repeat, following the instructions in Step 1.

Flower garden. Make several buttoned rosettes in different sizes. Instead of sewing fabric tails and affixing a bar pin, glue the rosettes to your card, adding felt or cut-ribbon stems and leaves.

Name:

Hello! Lucky

(Eunice Moyle and Sabrina Moyle)

Location: San Francisco, California, and London, United Kingdom

See page 45 for Hello!Lucky's complete bio.

rubber ducky, you're the one ADVANCED

you'll need

Rubber Ducky templates (Layers 1, 2, 3, 4, and 5)

Two 8¹/₂ x 11" sheets of tracing paper

Pencil, 2B or softer

Ballpoint pen

5 x 7" linoleum block (a woodblock works too; see Special Materials by Project, page 140.)

Utility knife

U-gouge carving tool (see Resources, page 139)

Ruler

Cutting mat, or a magazine

Two 11 x 17" sheets of heavy chipboard

Double-sided tape

Three 1¹/₄-oz jars of water-based block-printing ink (yellow, red, and black)

Cookie sheet or paper plate

Soft rubber brayer

6 to 7 sheets of printmaking paper (trimmed to 5 x 7")

Wooden spoon

Spray bottle filled with water (optional)

Wet sponge or cloth

Colored card stock (approximately 4 x 4")

Scallop-edged scissors

Scrap paper (optional)

Glue stick (optional)

Create this adorable ducky employing a technique known as reductive print, in which you print from the lightest color to the darkest, using the same wood or linoleum printing block. The first step is to carve away everything but the duck shape and print in your first color. Then, you carve away everything but the next-largest shaded area, and print in your second color. In the end, you are left with just the smallest area (in this case, the ducky's eye). Layering the ink gives you a rich, professional print that lends itself well to making multiples.

how to:

1 Trace and transfer the template.

Trace and transfer Layer 1 onto your printing block using tracing paper, a soft pencil, and a pen (see Trace and Transfer, page 138) (Figures 1–2). *Note: You are transferring the image backward on purpose—the block print will print the reverse of your image.*

2 Carve out the duck (Layer 1).

Using a utility knife, cut into the outline of the duck, leaving behind a continuous ¹/₈"-deep incision around the entire shape (Figure 3). Holding your U-gouge perpendicular to the incision and cutting toward the outline, carve away the area around the duck (Area 1). This should give you a nice clean line around the duck (Figure 4). Carve the remainder of Area 1. Always carve

away from you, holding the tool at a 45-degree angle in one hand and using your other hand to guide the tool and hold the block in place.

3 Assemble your printing station.

Using a ruler, utility knife, and cutting mat, cut out three pieces of chipboard: one 10 x 13" (this will be your backing board) and two strips that are 2 x 13" and 2 x 8". Position your backing board in landscape position, with the 13" side at the top. Using double-sided tape, tape the 2 x 13" strip along the long, upper side of your backing board, being careful to align the edges and corners. Tape the 2 x 8" strip along the shorter, left side of your backing board, butting it up against the longer strip to make a nice right angle (Figure 5). You'll use this as a guide for the placement of your printing block, so that it will be placed in the exact same spot every time (Figure 6).

4 Align your block.

Squeeze a small amount of yellow ink onto your cookie sheet. Use a brayer to roll out the ink into a nice even layer. Using the brayer, roll a thin layer of ink onto the duck shape of your block (Layer 1). Position the block on your printing station, butting the upper left corner of the block into the right angle you created with the chipboard strips (Figure 7). The block will be deeper than the chipboard guide you have created, so for the rest of the project, you'll align your paper to the upper left corner of the block.

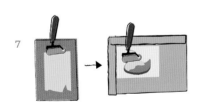

5 Print Layer 1.

Carefully align the upper left corner of a 5 x 7" sheet of printmaking paper to the upper left corner of the block. Then, firmly hold this corner in place with one hand while laying down the rest of the sheet with the other, making sure that the top edge of the paper aligns with the top edge of your block (Figure 8). Use the smooth, back side of a wooden spoon to rub the back of the paper onto the block, using firm, circular motions (Figure 9). If it is warm and dry outside, you might want to spray a little water on the paper before printing to keep the ink from drying too quickly. Repeat the printing process five or six times; you may need extra prints to accommodate mistakes as you continue. Also, consider the number of final prints you would like to have, and be sure to print enough to achieve this number. This is a reductive print, which means that you cut away more of the block with each color you print, so there is no going back once you've started carving the second color! When you are done printing Layer 1, set the cards aside to dry.

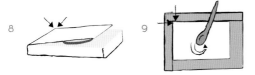

6 Carve Layer 2.

While Layer 1 is drying, clean off the block with a wet sponge or cloth (Figure 10). Trace and transfer Layer 2 onto the block. Carve away Area 2, again using a utility knife to first trace the outline of Layer 2 and then cutting up to that line using the U-gouge (Figure 11).

7 Print Layer 2.

Repeat Step 4, but this time, add a tiny dab of red to the yellow ink on your cookie sheet. Roll with your brayer until the ink is thoroughly mixed and you have a nice yellow that is a few shades darker than your first yellow. If you accidentally add too much red (not hard to do), simply add more yellow until you get the color you want. Repeat Step 5.

8 Carve and print the remaining colors.

Continue to carve and print, completing each of the three remaining areas.

You will carve and print the orange layer (Layer 3), then the red (the beak; Layer 4), and finally the black (the eye; Layer 5) (Figure 12).

12

9 Cut out the duck.

Once all the layers are dry, cut out your duck using a utility knife (Figure 13).

13

10 Create the scalloped background.

Place the colored card stock behind your duck. Using a pencil and ruler, mark out a rectangle on the card stock that is approximately 3 x 3 $^3/_4$", or a size that fits nicely behind the duck, allowing an extra $^1/_{16}$" all around the card to trim the scalloped edge. With a pair of scallop-edged scissors, trim the edges of the card (Figure 14). It's a good idea to practice on some scrap paper first, as it can be tricky to get the decorative corners to match up exactly.

14

11 Assemble the card.

Using double-sided tape or a glue stick, attach the scalloped background to the front of your card. Apply glue to the wrong side of your duck and position it so that it partially overlaps the scalloped background (Figure 15). Smooth to adhere.

15

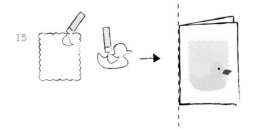

variations:

Print like the pros. If you want to do as real printmakers do, soak the print-making paper in your bathtub for a few minutes. Sandwich the wet paper between two sheets of blotter paper (see Resources, page 139) and firmly roll over it with a rolling pin or brayer, allowing the blotter paper to absorb the excess moisture. When your paper is damp to the touch, but not wet, it is ready to be printed on. Damp paper allows the inks to absorb better and results in a richer, more consistent print.

Baby duckies. The ability to make multiples means this project is perfect for birth announcements. Print as many ducklings as you'll need, and affix them assembly line–style to cards and backgrounds. Rubber-stamp the baby's name or birth date to the front of the card, and write the details inside. Use the same approach for a baby shower invitation.

You're the one! If your honey is familiar with that old *Sesame Street* tune ("Rubber Ducky, you're the one . . . "), affix the duck onto pink and/or red card stock. Rubber-stamp or write the words *You're the one* or *I'm certainly fond of you!* on the front of the card.

Name:

Pie Bird Press

(Hannah Berman)

Location: Berkeley, California

How did you get into crafting and/or card making? I studied printmaking in college and spent the majority of my time making linoleum block prints. After I graduated, I apprenticed with a letterpress printer, found that I could incorporate my blocks into stationery, and started my own business making cards.

What is your favorite medium? Carving linoleum and printing the blocks on my letterpress.

What is the most memorable card you've ever received (or sent)? One of my girlfriends made a valentine that had a homemade cookie in a little glassine pouch on the front. So cute!

What is your favorite card-sending occasion? My mother taught me to send thank you cards for every occasion, and I still do. It's so nice to get a note in the mail on a pretty card.

What is the one crafting tool you can't live without? My linoleum cutting blades, and I am also a sucker for ribbon.

What things most inspire your work? Years of flea market hunting and collecting, and all things shiny and colorful, like fireworks, glazed doughnuts, and holiday cookies.

What Web site is your favorite source of inspiration? www.etsy.com.

Where can we find you on the Web? www.wetfootpublications.com and http://printerpiemaker.blogspot.com.

fuzzy octopus valentine BASIC

you'll need

Glue stick

Pretty, patterned text-weight paper (trimmed to 4³/₄ x 6¹/₂")

Card stock (trimmed to 4³/₄ x 6¹/₂")

Right angle or ruler

Utility knife

Cutting mat, or a magazine

Corner rounder, or a glass to use as a guide for rounding corners (optional)

Pens

Fuzzy Octopus templates

Pencil

Tracing paper

4 straight pins

Felt (at least 7 x 7")

Scissors

Thread

Sewing needle

2 buttons

18" of embroidery floss

Embroidery needle

¹/₈" hole punch

3 to 4 pieces of 2 x 2" scrap paper in various colors

Fine-nibbed glue pen

This fuzzy felt card is a completely adorable way to let someone know you're a sucker for their friendship! The felt octopus's tentacles dangle alluringly off the edge of the card, and he has that sweet come-hither smile. Who could resist?

how to:

1 Make the card.

Apply glue to the wrong side of your patterned paper. Center your card stock on the patterned paper, and smooth to adhere (Figure 1). Using a right angle or ruler and a utility knife, trim the card down to 4¹/₂ x 6¹/₄" (Figure 2). If desired, round the corners using your corner rounder, or align the edge of a glass at each corner and cut around it using your utility knife.

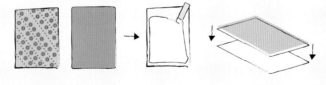

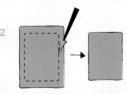

2 Write your message.

Write your message on the back of the card. We personally like *Sucker for you*, but feel free to get creative!

3 Cut out the octopus.

Using the template provided, trace the octopus onto a piece of tracing paper (Figure 3) (see Trace and Transfer, page 138). Pin the tracing paper to your felt using four straight pins. With the tracing paper as your guide, use a pair of scissors to cut out the octopus (Figure 4).

4 Make the face.

Make the eyes by sewing two buttons onto the felt (see Simple Sewing, page 137) (Figure 5). To create the mouth, hand-sew a curved line using the embroidery floss and embroidery needle and a backstitch (see Simple Sewing, page 137).

5 Add the suckers.

With your hole punch, punch about 10 dots from various colors of scrap paper (Figure 6). Using your fine-nibbed glue pen, squeeze a very small amount of glue onto the wrong side of one dot and adhere it to one of the octopus's tentacles. Repeat this process with the rest of your dots to create a smattering of suckers on all the tentacles.

6 Attach the octopus.

Using your glue stick, apply glue to the wrong side of the octopus and position it on your card (Figures 7–8). Smooth to adhere.

variations:

This card lends itself to all sorts of funny creatures and occasions. We suggest sticking with animals that will dangle off the edge of the card in some fashion.

Jellyfish. Cut a semicircle out of felt, and cut many 3 to 5" lengths of yarn to make the tentacles. Consider gluing or sewing a length of bric-a-brac along the bottom edge of the circle to simulate the curvy edge of the jellyfish's bell. Glue down the tentacles, letting them dangle off the edge of the card. Trim as necessary.

Many-eyed spider. Make a festive Halloween card by cutting an oval out of black felt and adding strips of black felt for legs. Glue down googly eyes, or sew on multiple buttons (the more the better!). Consider gluing down yarn or embroidery thread in the background to make a web.

Happy whale. Cut a whale shape out of felt. Glue a sprinkle of dots above it to represent a spray of water. Sew a smile on its face, and add a few lines of stitching to its belly for texture. This makes a great birthday, valentine, or every-day greeting card!

Name:
Daniel James

Location: San Francisco, California

How did you get into crafting and/or card making? My mother was an interior designer and consummate crafter—it seems to have rubbed off.

What is your favorite medium? Bits of felt and decorative papers.

What is the most memorable card you've ever received (or sent)? A cloth pirate ship was delivered unto me.

What is your favorite card-sending occasion? Valentine's Day. It's cheesy, but oh-so-delicious.

What is the one crafting tool you can't live without? Scissors, and a bit of glue.

What things most inspire your work? Pirates! Sea creatures, particularly octopi! Japanese paper and textiles.

What Web site is your favorite source of inspiration? www.deviantart.com.

Where can we find you on the Web? www.threerings.net and www.djames.org.

Kate Sutton

ahoy there! pop-up pirate card MODERATE

you'll need

Glue stick

2 pieces of lined notebook or filler paper (trimmed to 9 x 6¹/₄")

Card stock (trimmed to 9 x 6¹/₄")

Ruler

Bone folder

Scissors

Two 1¹/₂ x 9" strips of blue text-weight paper

Ahoy There templates

Two 8¹/₂ x 11" sheets of tracing paper

Pencil, 2B or softer

Ballpoint pen

Brown card stock or construction paper (trimmed to 9 x 6¹/₄")

Black pen

Two 4 x 4" scraps of red text-weight paper

Shiver me timbers! This card hails a pirate's hearty *ahoy!* to a friend, captain, or best mate. With its pop-up frigate and jolly sailin' birdies, it's sure to evince a mirthful demeanor from the scurvy lad or merry lass who receives it. Avast, me mateys, and anchors away!

how to:

1 **Line the card stock.**
Using your glue stick, apply glue to the wrong side of your first sheet of lined notebook paper. Center your card stock on the lined paper, and smooth to adhere. Repeat with your second sheet of lined paper and the other side of your card stock (Figure 1). With a ruler and bone folder, score and fold the card in half, parallel to the short side of your card (Figure 2).

2 **Make the waves.**
Cut wave shapes into a long side of one of the blue paper strips, either cutting freehand (Figure 3) or using the template provided. If you'll be using the template, trace and transfer the wave to your blue paper (see Trace and Transfer, page 138), and then trim it with scissors. Apply glue to the wrong side of the wave and adhere it to the front of your card, aligning the sides and bottom (Figure 3). Repeat with the second blue paper strip, pasting it to the back side of your card. Let it dry.

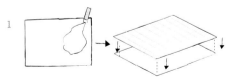

125

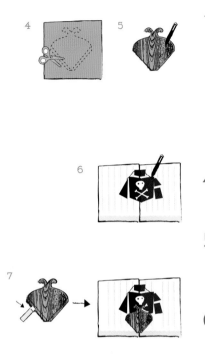

3 Make the boat.

Trace and transfer the Boat template to your brown card stock (Figure 4). Cut out the boat, using a pair of scissors. With your black pen, draw a wood-grain effect all over the front of the boat. Draw an almond-shaped or circular center forming the knot, then draw contour lines $1/4$" along the sides of the knot, echoing its shape and tapering to straight lines at either end; repeat the contour lines to form a striped wood grain pattern, adding additional knots as desired (Figure 5). Fold the boat in half, and then fold along the lines to create flaps, being sure both flaps fold away from you.

4 Draw a pirate sail.

Trace and transfer the Sail template (a pirate sail is also known as a Jolly Roger) to the upper half of your card. Color it in using a black pen (Figure 6).

5 Paste the boat in place.

With the boat facing right side up, apply glue to its flaps. Fold back and paste these flaps in place (just below the sail), pressing down on them to adhere (Figure 7).

6 Add a couple of pirate-y birds.

Trace and transfer the Bird template to your red paper, twice. Cut out two bird shapes (Figure 8). Apply glue to the wrong side of each bird and paste them in place on the card. Using a black pen, add features such as an eye patch and a pirate's hat (Figure 9).

7 Add your greeting.

Fold your card, and write a pirate-y greeting on the front, such as *Ahoy there!*

variations:

Avast, me hearties! Pirate lore and lingo are a fun starting point for a whole host of occasions. You may even consider giving this card to a friend on International Talk Like a Pirate Day (September 19)!

Best mate. Add the greeting *You're my best mate!* to let someone know you appreciate their friendship. Consider adding a cheery *Aarrr!* or *Aye, me hearty!* to the back of the card.

Pirate party. Use this card as an invitation to a pirate-themed party, or make it for the host if you are invited to one.

Anchors away! Give a merry send-off to a friend or colleague who is embarking on a new adventure. *Smooth sailin' an' fair winds t'ye!*

Name:

Kate Sutton

Location: Liverpool, United Kingdom

See page 33 for Kate Sutton's complete bio.

snail mail everyday note | BASIC

you'll need

Glue stick

Sheet of 9 x 12" children's newsprint writing paper (see Special Materials by Project, page 140)

Card stock, preferably pink (trimmed to $4^3/_4$ x $6^1/_2$")

Right angle or ruler

Utility knife

Cutting mat, or a magazine

Corner rounder, or a glass to use as a guide for rounding corners (optional)

Scissors

Newspaper or torn-out magazine page

Two or three $8^1/_2$ x 11" sheets of patterned or colored text-weight paper (optional)

Pencil, 2B or softer

4 x 6" pink text-weight paper

$8^1/_2$ x 11" sheet of tracing paper

Ballpoint pen

Snail Body template

4 x 6" green text-weight paper

Fine black felt-tip pen

Cutout newspaper, magazine, or computer-generated letters: *S-n-a-i-l M-a-i-l*, *T-o*, and *F-r-o-m*.

Send a pal a piece of bona fide snail mail with this adorable collage of colorful paper scraps, newspaper, and children's writing paper. Let this crafty snail deliver your message!

how to:

1 Make the card.

Apply glue to the wrong side of your newsprint paper. Center your card stock on the newsprint, and smooth to adhere (Figure 1). Using a right angle or ruler and a utility knife, trim the card down to $4^1/_2$ x $6^1/_4$" (Figure 2). If desired, round the corners using your corner rounder, or align the edge of a glass at each corner and cut around it using your utility knife.

2 Make the shell.

Cut a $2^1/_2$" circle out of the newspaper. Then, using your scissors, cut a spiral out of the circle: Starting along the outside edge of the circle, cut into the circle about $^1/_4$" and then make a continuous cut along the perimeter, working around it and progressively inward until you reach the center. From the outside edge, continuously trim off $^1/_8$" along the inside of the spiral, creating a narrow gap, until you reach the center (Figure 3). For a more colorful shell, photocopy a newspaper or magazine page onto a piece of colored text-weight paper, then cut out your spiral. You could also do this with your letters, photocopying them on several colors of paper for a mix-and-match look.

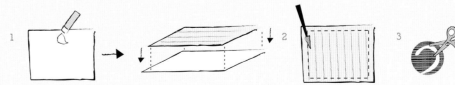

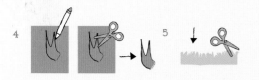

3 Make the body and grass.

With a pencil, draw the snail's body freehand on your pink paper, or trace and transfer the Snail Body template provided (see Trace and Transfer, page 138) and cut out with scissors (Figure 4). Cut a 1 x 3" strip of green paper. Using your scissors, cut fringe along one long side of this rectangle (Figure 5).

4 Assemble the card.

Glue the body, shell, and grass to the newsprint side of your card. Glue down the individual letters to make the message *Snail Mail* (Figure 6). Using your felt-tip pen, add a mouth and eyes to the snail (Figure 7).

5 Decorate the envelope.

Glue the letters *T-o* onto the front of the envelope and the letters *F-r-o-m* onto the flap. Fill in the recipient's address and then your own.

variations:

Slow but steady. Reunite with a long-lost friend. Replace the phrase *Snail mail* with *It's been too long* or *Snail's pace*. Write a funny note about how slow you've been to get back in touch. But, hey, slow and steady wins the race!

On the move! Make this card into a jolly moving announcement. Replace the phrase *Snail mail* with *On the move*. If you have kids, add a couple of smaller snails, perhaps stacking one on the back of the other. On the reverse side of the card, write or rubber-stamp your new address.

Belated birthday. Slow to remember a pal's birthday? Attach the letters *S-l-o-w p-o-k-e* to the front of the card. Consider giving the snail a party hat, made out of a triangle of colored or newsprint text-weight paper.

Name:

Hello!Lucky

(Eunice Moyle and Sabrina Moyle)

Location: San Francisco, California, and London, United Kingdom

See page 45 for Hello!Lucky's complete bio.

materials, tools and techniques

MATERIALS

PAPERS

Card stock
A thick paper stock. Also known as cover stock. Its thickness is described by pound weight or GSM (grams per square meter) and is generally available in 80 to 140 lb, or 100 to 400 GSM thicknesses. The best weight range for a nice card is 80 to 110 lb, or 200 to 300 GSM.

Chipboard
Inexpensive, stiff board often used for bookmaking and other projects that require rigidity. It is available at most art-supply and general craft stores.

Text-weight paper
A lighter weight paper; copy paper and writing paper are text-weight papers.

ADHESIVES

Craft glue
Water-based white glue that dries clear. It is nontoxic and can be cleaned up with soap and water, making it great for use with kids.

Double-sided adhesive film
A sheet of adhesive that has a removable backing on both sides, allowing you to turn anything into a sticker. Peel the backing from one side, and apply it to the first piece of paper. Then, peel off the backing from the other side, and stick your first piece of paper onto your second piece of paper.

Double-sided fusible web
Stabilizes fabric so that you can work with it like paper. Fusible web is made from a fabric that melts when heated. Double-sided fusible web comes with a pressure-sensitive coating on both sides; this enables you to adhere the web to your fabric, cut out your shapes, and then position and adhere the shapes to another piece of fabric or paper.

Drafting tape
Easily removable tape that does not leave a sticky residue when peeled off.

Glue pen
A fine-nibbed pen filled with glue, useful for adhering small things.

Glue stick
A solid adhesive that comes in a twist or push-up tube. It is great for working with papers, as it will not saturate paper or cause it to wrinkle or curl.

Hot-glue gun
An electric gun containing a heating element that melts plastic glue, which is sold in sticks.

Mod Podge
Paste glue that dries clear. It is nontoxic and can be cleaned up with soap and water, making it great for use with kids.

PVA glue
A water-based white glue. Widely used in bookbinding and book arts because of its flexibility and the fact that it is archival (pH neutral).

Spray adhesive
Glue that comes in a spray can. It is excellent for applying a thin coat of glue that will not saturate your paper or cause it to wrinkle or curl—also great for applying glue to delicate papers. Be sure to use spray adhesive in a well-ventilated area or outside. Also, it can get quite messy, so make sure to protect your work surface.

TOOLS

Awl
Small, pointed tool (looking a bit like a small ice pick) that can be used to punch little holes in papers. It also may be used as a pencil substitute when marking for cutting.

Bone folder
Bookbinder's tool used to crease and smooth folds, score and burnish paper, and work materials into tight corners. It is polished to a smooth finish to avoid damaging the paper or fabric it is drawn across.

Brayer
Small hand roller used to spread ink thinly and evenly. It is typically used in printmaking.

Circle cutter
Adjustable tool that allows you to cut perfect circles.

Clip art
Copyright-free artwork and alphabets, available in books and online (see Resources, page 139).

Corner rounder
A punch tool that rounds the corners of your paper.

Cutting mat
The best surface on which to use a utility knife. It is self-healing and will protect the blade of the knife. It's also typically marked with a ruled grid, handy for measuring and marking right angles.

Decorative paper punches
Punches are available in all sorts of shapes and sizes: variations on the classic hole punch, punches that make assorted shapes, and punches for cutting out fancy corners.

Decorative scissors
Decorative scissors have fancy-edged blades so that you can give paper scalloped or zigzagged edges.

Embossing tool
A tool with a round-tipped metal end used to press designs into paper.

Gocco (Print Gocco)
A simple, clean, self-contained printing system that allows you to make colorful prints at home.

Metal ruler
Safer and more accurate to use than a plastic ruler, these are available with a cork back to prevent slipping.

Photo reference
www.flickr.com is an excellent resource for looking up images to trace or draw from.

Tips:

Always have a fresh supply of blades on hand; dull blades will drag, creating a ragged edge.

Use a metal ruler when cutting with a utility knife; they are more accurate and safer to use than plastic rulers.

When cutting through thick paper, make several shallow cuts rather than a single deep one: It will be easier on your cutting hand, and the resulting cut will be crisp and clean.

Right angle ruler
Handy for making right angles. It is especially useful for scoring and folding a card in half without having to do a lot of measuring and marking.

Tracing paper
Translucent paper (also known as onion skin) that allows you to see the image you want to trace.

Utility knife or craft knife
Knife with a penlike body that holds a short, sharp, replaceable blade. It is exceptionally handy for making quick, accurate cuts.

Xyron machine
Tool for applying adhesive to the back of your paper. It essentially allows you to make a sticker out of anything. These machines are available in a variety of sizes, from 1" wide to $8\frac{1}{2}$ x 11" wide, at general craft stores.

TECHNIQUES

Accordion Fold

This is the fold you used in kindergarten for making fans and rows of gingerbread men; the resulting pleats resemble the bellows of an accordion, hence the name.

Start with a strip of paper. Fold a portion of the paper from left to right. Continue folding back and forth until you have folded the entire strip, and then use your bone folder to make strong creases.

Adding a Photo to a Card

Place the photo inside your card, and mark the top right and lower left corners with a pencil. Cut a slit diagonal to the two corners using a utility knife. Make the slits just wide enough that the photo corners will tuck in and hold the photo securely.

Clip-Art Transfer

You can transfer a clip-art image to any paper using a photocopy transfer.

you'll need:

Paper

Photocopy or black-and-white laser printout of artwork you want to transfer

Blender marker

how to:

1 Place the paper you are transferring the artwork to right side up on your work surface.

2 Place your artwork photocopy right side down on this paper.

3 Holding the photocopy in place with one hand, go over the area of your image with a blender marker, pressing firmly. Carefully lift one corner up to make sure that the image is transferring properly. Go over any areas that have not transferred completely.

Custom Rubber Stamps

Custom rubber stamps are inexpensive and handy for things like return addresses or blocks of text, particularly if you are making multiples. Additionally, you can create your own artwork, to be used in all kinds of creative ways. You can usually send your artwork to a rubber-stamp maker via e-mail or just supply them with a photocopy or black-and-white printout of your image (See Resources, page 139).

Double-Pasting

This technique allows you to neatly glue together two different types of paper so that they look like one sheet of double-sided paper. This is a great technique for creating cards that are patterned on the outside, but plain (and awaiting your clever missive) on the inside.

you'll need:

Two sheets of paper

Glue stick

Ruler

Utility knife

Cutting mat, or a magazine

how to:

1 Lay one piece of paper, wrong side up, on your work surface. Apply glue to the entire surface using a glue stick (Figure 1).

2 Center the second piece of paper, wrong side down, on the first piece of paper (Figure 2). Smooth to adhere.

3 With a ruler and utility knife, cut through both sheets of paper to the desired size (Figure 3).

4 Let it dry. (Stack several heavy books on top of your paper to ensure that it dries flat.)

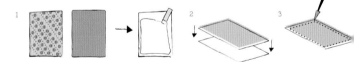

Lining an Envelope

you'll need:

2 envelopes

Ruler

Pencil

Utility knife or scissors

Cutting mat, or a magazine

Paper to use as liners (text-weight or lighter)

Glue stick or double-sided tape

how to:

1 Open your first envelope, and lay it flat.

2 Using a ruler and pencil, draw lines about ¹/₂" in from the edges of the flap (just inside the glue strip) and the sides, and about ¹/₁₆" above the bottom edge of the envelope (Figure 1). These lines will define the edges of your liner template.

3 Cut out the template you just created, using a ruler and utility knife or scissors (Figure 2).

4 Lay this template on your chosen liner paper. (If you are doing multiple envelope liners, you can lay your template on a stack of paper; you can cut though up to five sheets at once.) Cut around the template with the utility knife, using a ruler lined up with your envelope to give you a hard edge to cut against (Figure 3).

5 Slip the liner into your envelope and center it (Figure 4).

6 Holding the liner and envelope in place, fold the flap over and crease (Figure 5).

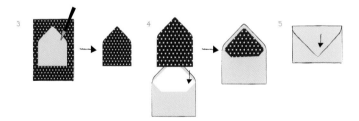

7 Lift the envelope flap, and apply glue or double-sided tape to the back of the liner flap (Figure 6).

8 Fold the envelope flap back down, smoothing to adhere it to the liner (Figure 7).

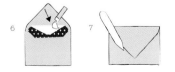

Making a Blank Card

you'll need:

Ruler

Card stock

Utility knife or scissors

Cutting mat, or a magazine

Pencil

Bone folder

how to:

1 Measure the height and width of your envelope. Double the side you want to fold (the short side for a vertical card, the long side for a horizontal card), and subtract ¹/₄" from both the length and width. This will be the size of your unfolded card. Trim down your card stock using these measurements.

2 Using your ruler and a pencil, make a mark halfway along the longest edge, both at the top and the bottom. Line up your ruler with these two marks, and run your bone folder along the edge of the ruler, pressing firmly. Fold your card along this score line, lining up the corners where they meet before creasing the paper.

Tip:

It helps to align your fold with the grain of the paper. To find the grain, fold a sheet of your card stock into quarters. One of the folds will be cleaner and neater than the other. This fold is running along the grain of the paper. Align your card measurements on the paper so that the fold will run along the grain.

Making Your Own Envelopes

Making your own envelopes allows for all kinds of fabulous results; you can make envelopes out of everything from pretty, patterned papers to pages from a magazine. Follow the instructions below to make your envelope entirely from scratch, using just a sheet of text-weight paper. You could also purchase an envelope template (available at craft stores) or take apart an envelope whose size and shape you like and use that as a template.

you'll need:

An envelope of any size, carefully torn open at the seams and laid flat, for guiding the shape of the envelope *(Note: If the envelope is the same size as your card, you could just trace this envelope to use as your template.)*

1 sheet of 8¹/₂ x 11" or 11 x 17" text-weight paper (depending on the size of your card)

Bone folder

Pencil or a pen if you are making envelopes from magazines

Ruler

Utility knife or scissors

Cutting mat or a magazine

Glue stick or double-sided tape

Remoistenable envelope glue (optional; available at many craft stores)

Mailing label (optional)

Stickers (optional)

how to:

1   Lay the text-weight paper on your work surface and place your card on it, centered from side to side and leaving more room at the top than the bottom (Figure 1).

2   Fold the bottom of the text-weight paper up and the top down, creasing the folds with a bone folder (Figure 2). Repeat for each side.

3   Unfold all four sides of the paper. You should be able to clearly see the dimensions of your card, along the folds. Use a pencil and ruler to mark the shape of the side, bottom, and top flaps, using your open envelope as a guide (Figure 3). Remember that the top flap should cover the side flaps and overlap the bottom flap.

4   Using a ruler and utility knife or scissors, cut out your envelope (Figure 4).

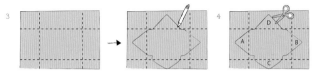

5   With your paper facing right side up, fold the side flaps (A and B) first, creasing them with a bone folder for a sharp fold. Next, fold the bottom flap (C), and crease. Unfold flap C and, with a glue stick, apply glue to it and fold up over flaps A and B, smoothing to adhere (Figure 5).

6   Fold the top flap (D), and crease (Figure 6). Apply envelope glue to the flap and let it dry, to be remoistened when you are ready to mail.

Alternatively, you can seal your envelope with glue, stickers, or a return address label. If you are using a magazine or other busy paper for your envelope, stick a mailing label on the front of the envelope for the address.

Metric Conversion Chart

Inches	Millimeters/Centimeters	Inches	Millimeters/Centimeters
¹/₈	3 mm	5	12.7 cm
³/₁₆	5 mm	5¹/₂	14 cm
¹/₄	6 mm	6	15.2 cm
³/₈	9.5 mm	6¹/₂	16.5 cm
¹/₂	1.3 cm	7	17.8 cm
⁵/₈	1.6 cm	7¹/₂	19 cm
³/₄	1.9 cm	8	20.3 cm
⁷/₈	2.2 cm	8¹/₂	21.6 cm
1	2.54 cm	9	22.9 cm
1¹/₂	3.8 cm	9¹/₂	24.1 cm
2	5 cm	10	25.4 cm
2¹/₂	6.4 cm	10¹/₂	26.7 cm
3	7.6 cm	11	27.9 cm
3¹/₂	8.9 cm	11¹/₂	29.2 cm
4	10.2 cm	12 (1 foot)	30.5 cm
4¹/₂	11.4 cm		

Rounding Corners

The easiest way to round corners is to use a punch, available at any general craft store. If you don't have a corner rounder handy, use the bottom of a glass. Line up the curve of the glass to the corner of your paper and, using the edge of the glass as your guide, trim off the corner of your paper using a utility knife. Alternatively, you can mark along the edge of your glass with a pencil and cut the corners using a pair of scissors.

SIMPLE SEWING

Straight Stitch

A straight stitch is the basic sewing stitch.

you'll need:

Thread

Sewing needle

Fabric or paper scraps for practicing

how to:

1 Tie a knot at the end of the thread, and thread your sewing needle.

2 Hold the threaded needle in your dominant hand; push the needle up through the back of your fabric (or paper), and pull until you hit the knot (Figure 1).

3 Reinsert the needle through the front of your fabric, a short distance from where it exited the fabric, and pull the thread all the way through (Figure 2).

4 Repeat (Figure 3).

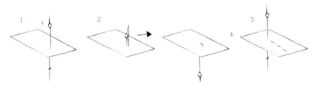

A speedy way to make a line of straight stitches (when you are not concerned about looks) is to accordion fold your fabric and run your needle through all the folds, pulling until you hit the knot at the end of your thread. When you pull your fabric flat, you'll have a row of stitches. This is also called a running stitch.

Backstitch

Backstitching is a method for making end-to-end stitches in a neat and tidy line; you do this by taking each stitch back to the end of the one you just made.

you'll need:

Threaded sewing needle

Fabric or paper scraps for practicing

how to:

1 Make a straight stitch (Figure 1).

2 Push the needle up from the back of your fabric to the front, moving about the length of your first stitch away from that stitch. Insert the needle into the hole made by the end of your first stitch (Figure 2).

3 Repeat Step 2.

Sewing on a Button

you'll need:

Button

Fabric or paper scraps for practicing

Threaded sewing needle

how to:

1 Hold your button against the fabric. With your threaded needle in your dominant hand, push the needle up through the back of your fabric through one of the holes in your button, and pull until you hit the knot at the end of your thread (Figure 1).

2 Reinsert the needle through the buttonhole diagonally opposite the one you started with, and pull the thread all the way through the fabric (Figure 2).

3 Repeat Steps 1 and 2, starting with one of the buttonholes next to the one your needle just went through, to form an *X* across the face of your button (Figure 3).

4 Tie a knot, and trim off the remaining thread (Figure 4).

Trace and Transfer

you'll need:

Tracing paper

An image you would like to transfer

Pencil, 2B or softer

Sheet of paper

Ballpoint pen

Light-colored chalk or pastel (optional)

how to:

1 Lay a piece of tracing paper over the image you would like to transfer, and trace it using your pencil (Figure 1).

2 Remove the tracing paper and place it facedown on the work surface. You should be able to see your tracing through the back of the tracing paper. Trace over it using your pencil (Figure 2).

3 Place the tracing paper on the paper you would like to transfer to, with your most recent tracing facedown (Figure 3). Hold your paper in place with one hand, and trace over the drawing with a ballpoint pen, pressing firmly. Carefully pull up one corner of the tracing paper to make sure that the drawing has transferred completely before removing it from your work.

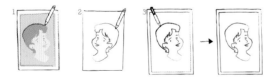

Tips:

If you are transferring to a dark surface, scribble over the entire second tracing with light-colored chalk or pastel before proceeding to Step 3 so you can see the transfer.

If you are transferring a drawing to a woodblock, use a light touch when going over the tracing with your ballpoint pen. The wood used for block printing is soft and will indent if too much pressure is used, resulting in a surface that will not ink up where the wood has been indented.

Wax Seals

Wax seals are a fabulous way to add a lovely, formal, and old-world feel to any project.

Traditional sealing wax comes in a stick with a wick. Light the wick with a lighter or match and allow the melting wax to drip onto your surface, forming a small puddle. Press your seal into the wax, and set the wax aside to cool and harden.

Glue-gun sealing wax is the modern-day version of sealing wax. It is especially useful when you are working on a large project. The sticks of wax will fit into any standard-size glue gun and are available in a wax that resembles genuine sealing wax.

Seals are available in a variety of motifs, or you can have one custom made.

Writing on Dark Papers

Use a gel pen to write on dark papers; gel pens come in many light shades and are opaque. They are also available with glittery inks.

Resources

The artists who have contributed to this book hail from the United States and Europe; given the popularity of card crafting on both sides of the pond, whenever possible we have included both U.S. and U.K. resources for finding the materials you'll need.

General Craft and Art Supplies

The Art of Craft: www.art-of-craft.co.uk

Calico Crafts: www.calicocrafts.co.uk

Crescent Quilling: www.crescentquilling.co.uk

Daniel Smith: www.danielsmith.com

Dick Blick Art Materials: www.dickblick.com

Flax Art and Design: www.flaxart.com

Graphic Discount: www.graphicdiscount.co.uk

London Graphic Centre: www.londongraphics.co.uk

Michaels: www.michaels.com

Millers: www.millers-art.co.uk

Paper Source: www.paper-source.com

Pearl Paint: www.pearlpaint.com

ScrapMagic: www.scrapmagic.com

Utrecht Art Supplies: www.utrechtart.com

Paper

See also General Craft and Art Supplies *and* Ecofriendly Papers.

Craftwork Cards: www.craftworkcards.co.uk

Creative Papers Online: www.handmade-paper.us

French Paper Company: www.mrfrench.com

GF Smith (envelopes): www.gfsmith.com

Paper Zone: www.paperzone.com

Decorations and Specialty Supplies

See also General Craft and Art Supplies. *Local flea markets are also great places to find vintage fabrics, ribbons, and ephemera for your projects.*

The Button Queen (vintage buttons): www.thebuttonqueen.co.uk

Cavellini & Co. (rubber stamps and decorative papers): www.cavellini.com

Crafts U Love (scrapbooking supplies): www.craftsulove.co.uk

Impress Rubber Stamps (rubber stamps and inks): www.impressrubberstamps.com

Library of Congress (maps): www.loc.gov/shop

Nostalgic Impressions (wax seals): www.nostalgicimpressions.com

Oriental Trading Company (scrapbooking, novelty, and crafting supplies): www.orientaltrading.com

Raffit Ribbon (ribbons and trims): www.raffit.com

Sierra Enterprises (rubber stamps and inks): www.sierra-enterprises.com

Sir Stampalot (rubber stamps and inks): www.sirstampalot.co.uk

Tinsel Trading Company (vintage-inspired ribbons, embellishments, and novelty supplies): www.tinseltrading.com

VV Rouleaux (ribbons and trims): www.vvrouleaux.com

Ecofriendly Papers

See also Paper *and* General Craft and Art Supplies.

Cutting Edge Cards: www.eco-craft.co.uk

The Exotic Paper Company: www.elliepoopaper.co.uk

Greenfield Paper Company: www.greenfieldpaper.com

The Green Stationery Company: www.greenstat.co.uk

Fabric

Cath Kidston: www.cathkidston.co.uk

Cia's Palette: www.ciaspalette.com

The Cotton Patch: www.cottonpatch.co.uk

Fat Quarter Shop: www.fatquartershop.com

Jo-ann Fabric and Crafts: www.joann.com

Liberty of London: www.libertyoflondon.co.uk

Purl: www.purlsoho.com

Repro Depot: www.reprodepot.com

Super Buzzy: www.superbuzzy.com

Z & S Fabrics: www.zandsfabrics.com

Art

The British Library, Picture Library—Images Online: www.imagesonline.bl.uk

Clipart.com: www.clipart.com

CSA Images: www.csaimages.com

Dover Publications: www.doverpublications.com

Flickr (for photo reference): www.flickr.com

Jupiter Images: www.jupiterimages.com

My Fonts: www.myfonts.com

The Pepin Press: www.pepinpress.com

Special Materials by Project

You can find the materials needed to make the projects in this book in innumerable places, from around the house to your local flea market or craft store; the more you can put your own stamp on the project, the better! That said, if want to find the exact material or notion shown in the photo (or something very similar), you should try the following resources.

Pop-Up Birdie Hello (page 31)

U.S. no. 10 (European DL—110 x 220 mm) end-opening envelope from Paper Source (see General Craft and Art Supplies) and World of Envelopes (www.worldofenvelopes.com) respectively.

Wood You Be Mine? Valentine (page 35)

Balsa wood (4 x $^3/_{16}$ x 36" sheets) from Pearl Paint (see General Craft and Art Supplies) or 4D Model Shop (www.yellowcatshop.co.uk).

Clip art (see Art).

Lacy Paper Notes (page 43)

Similar paper doilies from My Paper Shop (www.mypapershop.com) or the Cook's Kitchen (www.thecookskitchen.com).

Custom rubber stamps from Impress Rubber Stamps (see Decorations and Specialty Supplies) or the English Stamp Company (www.english customstamps.com).

Magical Birthday Banner (page 47)

$3^1/_2$ x $2^1/_2$" papier mâché minibox from Dick Blick Art Materials (see General Craft and Art Supplies) or Calico Crafts (see General Craft and Art Supplies).

Clip art (see Art).

Music-box mechanism (musical movement) from Craft Supplies Online (www.craft-supplies-online.com) or Music Box World (www.deanorgans.co.uk).

Sparkly Thank You Bouquet (page 53)

Craft glue with ultrafine metal tip attachment and glitter from Art Institute Glitter (www.artglitter.com) or the Glitter Pot (www.theglitterpot.co.uk).

Embossed Stencil Correspondence Card (page 59)

Drafting tape from Dick Blick Art Materials (see General Craft and Art Supplies) or London Graphic Centre (see General Craft and Art Supplies).

Embossing tool from Lasting Impressions (www.lastingimpressions.com) or the Art of Craft (see General Craft and Art Supplies).

Brass embossing stencils from Celebration (www.brass-stencils.com) or the Art of Craft (see General Craft and Art Supplies).

Silhouette Save the Date (page 63)

Screen-printing supplies, including screen-printing unit, photo emulsion, photo sensitizer, screen-printing ink, and photoflood lightbulbs, from Dick Blick Art Materials (see General Craft and Art Supplies) or London Graphic Centre (see General Craft and Art Supplies).

Custom-made screens from Standard Screen Supply (www.standardscreen.com).

Arturo cover-weight paper in pale blue (12 x 12") from Paper-Papers.com (www.paperpapers.com).

Script font (Archive Penman Script) from My Fonts (see Art).

Library Book Birth Announcement (page 71)

Library card pockets from Teaching Supply Store (www.teachingsupply store.com) or Gresswell (www.gresswell.com).

Animal Print Everyday Note (page 81)

Print Gocco machine and supplies from Northwood Studios (www.northwoodstudios.tripod.com) or Paper Source (see General Craft and Art Supplies); for additional suppliers, visit www.savegocco.com/resources.html.

Little Accordion Card (page 85)

Small mailing or gift box from Paper Mart (www.papermart.com) or All Boxed Up (www.all-boxed-up.co.uk).

A Thoughtful Gesture Thank You Note (page 191)

Print Gocco machine and supplies from Northwood Studios (www.northwoodstudios.tripod.com) or Paper Source (www.paper-source.com); for additional suppliers, visit www.savegocco.com/resources.html.

Clip art (see Art).

Photo Ornament Holiday Card (page 103)

Wooden ornament/gift tag from Lara's Crafts (www.larascrafts.com), Calico Crafts (see General Craft and Art Supplies), or Kipper Workshop Country Crafts (www.kipperworkshops.com or http://stores.ebay.co.uk/kipper-workshop-crafts). *(Note: If a predrilled tag is not available, look for plain tags and a minidrill, available at many craft stores.)*

Baker's twine (and other thin, pretty ribbon) from Raffit Ribbon (see Decorations and Specialty Supplies) or the Ribbon Company (www.the ribboncompany.com).

Big Number Birthday Card (page 107)

4" number stencil from Pearl Paint (see General Craft and Art Supplies) or the Stencil Warehouse (www.stencilwarehouse.com). Wood sorrel rubber stamp from Paper Source (see General Craft and Art Supplies).

Acetate or Mylar from Dick Blick Art Materials (see General Craft and Art Supplies) or London Graphic Centre (see General Craft and Art Supplies).

Blue-Ribbon Badge Congratulations Card (page 111)

1" bar pin with safety catch from Connecticut Laminating Company (www.ctlaminating.com) or Clere Identities Limited (www.clere-identities.co.uk).

Rubber Ducky, You're the One (page 115)

Block-printing supplies, including blotting paper, linoleum block, and three-ply Shina plywood woodblock from Dick Blick Art Materials (see General Craft and Art Supplies), McClain's Printmaking Supplies (www.imcclains.com), or London Graphic Centre (see General Craft and Art Supplies).

Snail Mail Everyday Note (page 129)

Children's newsprint writing paper from Teacher's Supply (www.teacherssupply.com).

Index

Acknowledgments

Our warm thanks go first to the 22 guest artists who contributed the wonderful projects found on these pages. We are honored to be in the company of such talented, innovative, independent card makers and look forward to creative camaraderie and mutual encouragement for many years to come.

Thanks, too, to the staff of Hello!Lucky who contributed to the writing, editing, and illustrating of this book. Sarah Labieniec created the wonderfully expressive how-to illustrations that accompany each project. Lauren Ottaviano tirelessly edited and project-tested, in addition to collecting artists' biographies and serving, with Jennifer Vencill and Nicholas Hurd, as a card-making tools and techniques expert. Chlöe Greene, Chun Yee Yip O'Neill, Shauna Leytus, and Kelly Dorrance provided creative direction and recommendations on artists to include in the book and also helped collect (and protect) project samples. Kelly Rector, our resident wit, helped craft the introduction and reviewed many a project. Mary Wong kept everything running smoothly while we focused on this book. Karin Olsson, Hana Lee, Alexa Calos, and Joanne Ferrell provided invaluable input and support.

We are also grateful to Kate Prouty and Jodi Warshaw, our brilliant editors at Chronicle Books. Thank you for your support and for recognizing the refreshing burst of creativity that so many of today's artists bring to the card-making craft.

Finally, thank you to Julian for nurturing our dream of starting a little card company from the very beginning. We are grateful for your patience, candor, and encouragement.